Louis XIV

David L. Smith

*Fellow of Selwyn College,
Cambridge*

CAMBRIDGE
UNIVERSITY PRESS

Published by the Press Syndicate of the University of Cambridge
The Pitt Building, Trumpington Street, Cambridge CB2 1RP
40 West 20th Street, New York, NY 10011–4211, USA
10 Stamford Road, Oakleigh, Melbourne 3166, Australia

© Cambridge University Press 1992

First Published 1992

Reprinted 1995

Printed in Great Britain by Bell & Bain Ltd, Glasgow

A catalogue record for this book is available from the British Library.

ISBN 0 521 40699 4

Maps by Jeff Edwards

NOTICE TO TEACHERS

GO

Contents

Acknowledgements

I am greatly indebted to John Morrill for his unfailing help, advice and encouragement throughout the preparation of this book. Richard Brown also commented on draft chapters and made many valuable suggestions. I wish to thank the staff at Cambridge University Press, and especially Stephanie Boyd, for their assistance, courtesy and professionalism. This book was conceived, researched and written during my time as a Research Fellow of Selwyn College, Cambridge. I am deeply grateful to the Master and Fellows for electing me to a post which enabled me to undertake the project in such a stimulating and congenial environment. I dedicate this book to them, in appreciation.

The author and publishers would like to thank the following for permission to reproduce copyright material:

1.4 'Reflections on the Role of King', in *A King's Lessons in Statecraft*, ed. J. Longnon, trans. H. Wilson, Fisher Unwin; 2.12, 2.13, 4.15, 6.3 J. Lough (ed.), *Locke's Travels in France*, Cambridge University Press; 2.16 M.B. Curran (ed.), *The Despatches of William Perwich*, Boydell & Brewer Ltd; 7.1 R. Briggs, *Early Modern France, 1560–1715*, by permission of Oxford University Press; 7.2 J.B. Wolf (ed.), *Louis XIV: A Profile*, Macmillan; 7.3 F. Bluche, *Louis XIV*, Librairie Arthème Fayard; 7.4 D.H. Pennington, *Europe in the Seventeenth Century*, Longman Group UK Ltd; 7.5 T. Munck, *Seventeenth-Century Europe: State, Conflict and the Social Order in Europe, 1598–1700*, Macmillan; 7.6 R. Mettam, *Power and Faction in Louis XIV's France*, Basil Blackwell; 7.7 J. Miller, 'Introduction', in *Absolutism in Seventeenth-Century Europe*, ed. J. Miller, Macmillan; 7.8 R. Lockyer, *Habsburg and Bourbon Europe, 1470–1720*, Longman Group UK Ltd; 7.9 J.H. Shennan, *Louis XIV*, Methuen & Co; 7.10 J.S. Morrill, 'French Absolutism as Limited Monarchy', *Historical Journal* XXI, 1978, Cambridge University Press.

Illustrations: 6.9, 6.11, 6.12 and 6.13 Cliché des Musées Nationaux, Paris; 6.10 Aerofilms Limited; 6.15 Bibliothèque Nationale, Paris; 6.17 Photographie Giraudon; 6.19 Robert W. Berger.

Cover illustration: *Louis XIV* by Hyacinthe Rigaud, 1701, AKG London.

Introduction

A   The problem

King Louis XIV of France ranks as one of the most remarkable monarchs in history. He reigned for seventy-two years, longer than any other modern European ruler. For fifty-four of these he personally controlled French government; and his power and influence have prompted scholars to label the later seventeenth century 'the age of Louis XIV'. His name is also given to a period of furniture and a style of architecture. The palace which he built at Versailles became the envy of other monarchs throughout Europe. Dubbed the 'Sun-King' during his own lifetime, his rule has since been hailed as the supreme example of a type of government – 'absolutism'. Among contemporaries and later historians alike, he has aroused lavish praise and bitter condemnation. Nevertheless, whether they loved or loathed him, when Louis XIV died very few of his subjects could remember any other monarch.

Yet, despite this astonishing fame, and the massive quantity of evidence relating to Louis's life, many aspects of his political career remain mysterious. What were his aims, and how successful was he in achieving them? What was the nature of his social, economic and religious policies? Did he sacrifice the interests of his people for the sake of foreign wars? Was his reign a period of change and reform, or of inertia and stagnation? And what were his lasting achievements, and his legacy to France and Europe? We shall examine these and many other questions throughout the chapters which follow. The documents and commentary are designed to help you formulate answers of your own.

Louis's reign was extremely long and this book is relatively short. It therefore makes sense to concentrate on the period after 1661, when Louis assumed personal control of French government. The purpose of this Introduction is briefly to provide some background on French history before that date (Section B); to review the main areas of debate over Louis's career (Section C); and finally to explain the structure and contents of the book (Section D). This chapter, like the others, is designed for use alongside other works. It does not provide a comprehensive treatment of Louis XIV, but assumes that you already have an outline knowledge of his career and some sense of events in France during his lifetime. These may be gained from any of the surveys listed in the Bibliography on pp. 125–30.

B   Background and context

In order to understand Louis's career after 1661, we must first place it in the context of French history during the early and mid-seventeenth century. Louis was born on 5 September 1638, the eldest son of King Louis XIII (1610–43) and Anne of Austria, Queen of France. His parents' marriage had been childless for over twenty years, and the birth of a male heir was hailed as a gift from God. The baby became known as 'Louis le Dieudonné' ('Louis the God-given'). Yet behind the rejoicing, the ringing of church bells and the services of thanksgiving, there lay an uneasy sense that all was not well in France.

Since 1635 Louis XIII had been fighting a two-front war against the Habsburg rulers of Spain and the Holy Roman Empire. This conflict, fought to protect French territory from Habsburg encirclement, had been engineered by Cardinal Richelieu, Louis's chief minister. From the late 1620s until his death in 1642, Richelieu dominated French politics. But the war necessitated massive increases in taxation, causing a series of popular revolts during the later 1630s and early 1640s. Louis XIV was only four-and-a-half years old when his father died in May 1643, and his mother was therefore declared Queen Regent, with the Italian Cardinal Mazarin as chief minister. As the war dragged on and economic conditions deteriorated, pamphlets known as Mazarinades denounced Anne of Austria and Mazarin, and even accused them of deliberately prolonging the conflict. The Peace of Westphalia (24 October 1648) ended the war against the Emperor; but the quarrel with Spain showed no sign of being resolved. Finally, in the summer of 1648, France's chief law court, the *parlement* of Paris (see Chapter 3), insisted that it had a right to be consulted over major decisions of state.

This example was followed by many provincial *parlements* and triggered five years of civil war known as the 'Frondes' (after the catapults used by Parisian children). France soon faced a general tax-strike, and the government entirely lacked the machinery to compel payment. In 1650, the princes of the blood (members of the royal family) also demanded a say in government and the removal of 'evil advisers'. Led by the Prince de Condé, they took up arms in 1650. These dramatic events coincided with several catastrophic harvests and an outbreak of plague. Hunger drove some to gnawing roots, grass and even their own limbs. Twice, in 1649 and 1651, uprisings in Paris forced the royal court to flee to country palaces. Eventually, during 1652–3, the King's forces under Turenne quelled the provincial rebellions, defeated Condé, and regained control of Paris.

Perhaps the most significant effect of the Frondes was the impact which it made on the young Louis XIV. He never forgot the collapse of public order and the shock of twice having to leave Paris. His later policies – his suspicion of the *parlements* [3.5–3.6], his desire to tame the nobility [3.1–3.4], and his search for firm monarchical government [1.1–1.4] – can only be explained in the context of the disastrous political breakdown which he had witnessed as a boy. (Boldface numbers in square brackets refer to the documents in Chapters 1–7.)

Although Louis had legally come of age in September 1651, this actually changed the distribution of power very little. Anne of Austria, though no longer regent, remained leader of the Council of State after the King, while Mazarin was still chief minister. After 1653 royal powers were gradually consolidated, and France slowly gained the upper hand in the war against Spain. The Peace of the Pyrenees (6 June 1659) gave France several important strategic sites and effectively marked Spain's eclipse as the leading power in Europe. The new peace was symbolised by Louis XIV's marriage to the Spanish King's daughter Marie-Thérèse on 9 June 1660.

Mazarin did not attend the lavish ceremony: he was already seriously ill, and died on 9 March 1661. Louis then took the crucial decision not to appoint another chief minister, but to assume direct control over French government himself [1.1]. So began the 'personal rule' of Louis XIV which was to last until his own death in September 1715. He took the reins of a kingdom which had still not fully recovered from the Frondes, but which was now at peace and whose economy was becoming steadily stronger. It was, perhaps, a kingdom ripe for the assertion of royal authority.

C Areas of debate

Five aspects of Louis's career after 1661 have proved particularly controversial: his personality and motives; the extent to which his régime was 'absolutist'; his policies and priorities in government; how far his reign was a period of change or of continuity; and the nature of his achievements and legacy. Let us take each of these in turn.

1   Character, mind and motives

What sort of a person was Louis XIV? Historians have disagreed sharply about his character and the extent to which he possessed any special qualities. The only attribute which all would recognise is his physical strength [7.1]. Any monarch who personally ruled a major European state for fifty-four years, and who survived a string of illnesses – including smallpox, an operation for an anal fistula (ulcer), and a tooth extraction which brought away part of his upper jaw as well – clearly possessed immense stamina. Furthermore, contemporary observers invariably remarked upon Louis's vitality and energy [1.14; 6.2; 6.3; 6.6].

But on two other issues there is no such consensus. First, it is far from clear whether Louis was of more than average intelligence. On the one hand, Robin Briggs has found him 'mediocre . . . in many respects' [7.1]. But on the other, François Bluche has recently laid down a fundamental challenge: how could any man 'of mediocre intelligence' possibly have achieved all that Louis did [7.3]? It may be, however, that different historians use the term 'intelligence' in different ways. It seems unlikely that Louis was academically distinguished: the cast of his mind was practical rather than theoretical. But that does not preclude a powerful political intelligence and insight. In the chapters which follow, you will be able to read many extracts from Louis's own writings, and draw your own conclusions from them.

A similar disagreement exists over whether Louis possessed any firm political principles. His enemies accused him of ruthless ambition and lack of scruple [5.4–5.5]. They saw him as a pragmatist who reacted to circumstances and had no consistent goal except his own self-aggrandisement. Conversely, it has been argued that Louis always wished to safeguard France's national interests as he understood them [7.8]. Yet there is, perhaps, no necessary incompatibility between these two interpretations. The prestige of seventeenth-century states was so closely linked to the personal reputations of their rulers that Louis's own pursuit of 'glory' [1.3; 5.2] was almost bound to affect France's standing within Europe. As Louis realised [1.4], he could therefore serve himself and his country without any sense of inconsistency.

These questions matter because seventeenth-century France was very much a 'personal monarchy' in which the king's character, beliefs and wishes had a direct effect on official policy. From 1661, the King ruled as well as reigned. Only by getting Louis's personality straight, therefore, can we penetrate to the heart of his régime and of political processes during his reign.

2 Absolutism

This brings us to the second controversy, which concerns the extent to which Louis XIV was an 'absolute' monarch. The debate is extremely complex, but essentially it revolves around three key questions: what do we mean by 'absolutism' and 'absolute' power; did Louis covet such 'absolute' power for himself; and, whether he wanted to or not, how far did he actually achieve it?

First, the major problem of definition. The word 'absolutism' only became a political term in France after 1789, and in England during the 1830s. The phrase 'absolute monarchy' appeared in the seventeenth century, but contemporaries differed dramatically in their use of it. You will see below how one of Louis's leading subjects, Bishop Bossuet, defined 'absolute government' [1.7]. He thought it both defensible and desirable; yet for others, including the English philosopher Thomas Hobbes, 'absolutism' was a term of abuse. The historiographical debate has been bedevilled by a similar failure to define terminology. No modern definition will be perfect; but perhaps we grasp the essentials if we apply it to a system of hereditary monarchy where the kings or queens are not answerable to any earthly authority because their right to rule is thought to derive from God alone, but where they nevertheless have a moral obligation to exercise power according to Christian principles rather than their own whim.

That said, how far did Louis XIV seek such power? Historians are divided over whether Louis possessed a concept of 'absolutism', and if so, how far this guided his political actions. Some would see him as 'conservative by temperament' [7.6], while others are more impressed by Louis's dynamism, energy and drive for innovation [7.9; 7.10]. In the course of this book, you will be able to examine Louis's own analysis of the powers and duties of king [1.1–1.4]; and later to compare this with contemporary accounts of his behaviour [6.2; 6.6].

Finally, does the term 'absolutism' accurately describe Louis XIV's régime? On balance, most historians writing over the last forty years have been struck more by the limitations on royal authority than by the power of the French crown [7.4–7.7]. They point to the continuing privileges of particular social groups and geographical regions [3.1–3.3; 3.14]; to the role of the legal courts (especially the *parlements*) in frustrating royal policies [3.8]; to the failure of the Crown to resolve religious disputes (see Chapter 4); and above all to the insurmountable obstacles posed by the combination of a very big country and a very small bureaucracy [1.16–1.18].

Although these arguments are very telling, it is important not to forget that royal powers did increase considerably in seventeenth-century France [7.10]. Moreover, as John Miller has recently reminded us, 'it would be naïve to expect twentieth-century standards of efficiency... of a seventeenth-century administration' (see the introduction to his collection cited in the Bibliography on page 127). Insofar as Louis achieved a degree of royal control which was unusual by the standards of his time, he might still fairly be described as 'the great exemplar' of absolutism in practice (see the article by J.H. Burns in Miller's collection).

We will encounter these issues of royal power and authority again and again throughout this book. But to clarify the problems further, the whole of Chapter 1 is devoted to 'absolutism' in both theory and practice. There you will be able to assess the judgements of historians [7.4–7.7] in the light of a selection of original evidence.

3   Policies and priorities

Before we discuss Louis's policies and priorities as king, it is necessary to sound a note of caution. In the late twentieth century, we think of 'policy' as something planned, co-ordinated and controlled by central government. But in the early modern period, limited administrative and economic resources imposed major constraints on a ruler's ability to implement coherent policies. The vast majority of historians working on the period would accept this general point. Where they would part company is over how far Louis's various policies displayed common features; and over the extent to which they contradicted or reinforced each other.

One very influential line of argument places 'glory' at the heart of Louis's concerns [7.8]. Certainly Louis frequently expressed a desire to attain '*la gloire*' [1.3], and asserted that this could be achieved in a variety of ways – through religious policies [4.11] as well as through diplomacy and war [5.1; 5.2]. This highlights an underlying unity and coherence within Louis's policies, and suggests that his different avenues of policy were all directed towards the same ultimate goal.

Against this, many scholars have stressed the incompatibility of Louis's objectives. In particular, it is argued that his obsessive pursuit of war impeded domestic reform [7.7] and impoverished the French people [7.9]. Louis sacrificed the success of his social and economic policies for the sake of military campaigns and foreign conquests. This view was also voiced by some of Louis's contemporaries [2.17]. There is even a legend that on his deathbed Louis regretted his choice of priorities as king, and lamented that 'I have loved war too much'.

But these two interpretations may not be mutually exclusive. In this period, foreign policy was seen as the natural sphere of monarchs (see Chapter 5), and it is therefore unsurprising if Louis thought that success in war conferred more 'glory' than domestic harmony and prosperity. Thus, his pursuit of 'glory' might itself explain why he made foreign policy his top priority. Nevertheless, it is difficult to see how this outlook could have permitted comparable success in other areas of policy. Something or someone had to suffer, as several of the extracts demonstrate [2.13–2.17].

4 Change and continuity

The fourth debate concerns the extent to which France changed during Louis XIV's reign. All historical enquiry involves the analysis of change over time, the evaluation of how and why some elements in the past altered while others remained the same. But this is particularly a theme of French history. As Alphonse Karr said of French politics in 1849, 'the more it changes, the more it is the same thing' ('plus ça change, plus c'est la même chose').

How far was this true of France under Louis XIV? The drift of research since 1945 has been to play down the speed and scale of changes during his reign. Numerous scholars have emphasised how many aspects of French politics, government and society remained essentially unaltered. They stress the lack of fundamental administrative and institutional reform at both central and local levels [7.6; 7.7]. The venality of office (whereby monarchs sold certain public positions) continued to be a major obstacle to reform, particularly because these offices could become hereditary on payment of an annual tax known as the *paulette* [7.7]. The personnel of government remained largely unchanged [7.6]. Little was done to tackle the problem of debt; indeed this became much worse during the course of the reign [2.5]. All these basic structural weaknesses of the French monarchy were not corrected until after the revolution of 1789. The forces of continuity thus obstructed any fundamental alterations which Louis XIV sought.

But there is an alternative to this view of stagnation. A number of historians have focused on the ways in which Louis XIV's rule differed from that of his predecessors [7.3; 7.9; 7.10]. They stress that he eroded entrenched social, regional and legal privileges. He made noble status open to merchants and other enterprising individuals [3.1–3.4]; he reduced provincial autonomy [1.8–1.10; 3.9; 3.10]; and curbed the powers of the law courts [3.5; 3.6]. Louis tightened his control over the Church and finally resolved the long-standing problem of France's Protestant minority (see Chapter 4). The machinery of state became heavily involved in new areas, such as the patronage of the arts [6.9–6.19]. Louis also broke new ground as a politician: he realised the central importance of public display [6.1–6.3] and made more use of visual propaganda than any previous French monarch [4.17; 5.10]. In all these ways, Louis's policies and political style marked a significant departure from what had gone before.

It is difficult to accept either of these arguments in isolation, and Louis's reign probably saw a complex interaction between the forces of change and those of continuity. But where you would place the greatest emphasis – whether you are more impressed by the impetus to reform or by the constraints upon it – is for you to decide from the original sources which follow.

5 Achievements and legacy

Finally, what did Louis XIV achieve, and what is his place in history? In one sense, his impact seems beyond doubt. Whether an 'absolute' monarch or not, he clearly wielded immense powers and decisively affected the military and political history of Europe during his lifetime. Had he not lived, the late seventeenth and early eighteenth centuries would have looked very different.

Many historians have gone further than this, and argued that a large number of his achievements outlived him. They have emphasised that the frontiers of France have scarcely changed since Louis's death; that her political, military and cultural ascendancy within Europe increased dramatically during his reign; and that he created a far more powerful state machinery than had existed before [7.8; 7.9]. During the seventeenth century, the French monarchy greatly increased its control over administration, justice, taxation, culture and religious life [7.10]. France emerged stronger, more united and more influential in 1715 than she had been in 1661. All this apparently justifies J.H. Shennan's description of Louis XIV as 'one of the architects of modern France' [7.9].

Another approach, while not denying Louis's achievements, would want to qualify them heavily. Donald Pennington has called the reign 'a story . . . of mitigated disaster' [7.4]. He exemplifies those scholars who believe that Louis's legacy was vitiated by his love of war, and that he would have achieved far more if he had pursued a less bellicose foreign policy. He left behind one of the most famous names in history; but we look in vain for concrete or lasting changes in French society and government. The human and financial cost of his wars was massive, and he left France exhausted and burdened with debt [7.7].

But in the end, this debate over Louis's achievements and legacy does not make his career any less worth studying. Whether or not he set France on the path to modernity, he was undeniably someone who dominated his world, and decisively affected the course of political and military developments during his lifetime. However many blemishes appear on our picture of the 'Sun-King', Cornelio Bentivoglio, papal agent at the French Court, was surely correct when he wrote that Louis's name 'will live on in the history of the centuries to come, and it will be difficult to find his equal again'.

D   Sources and themes

The documents and commentary in this book are intended to help you form your own opinions about these controversial issues. The 131 extracts and illustrations are inevitably a very small selection from the vast body of evidence relating to Louis XIV's life and career which has come down to us. Louis XIV is one of the best documented figures in all history. The available sources include Louis's own letters and memoirs; official documents generated by central government; private diaries and correspondence; contemporary tracts, pamphlets, sermons and poems; original paintings, coins and medals; and the physical evidence of Louis's palaces and gardens. Examples from each of these categories appear in this book.

Throughout, two aims have determined my selection of material. First, I have tried to balance extracts from Louis's own words and from official sources against the accounts and descriptions left by his contemporaries. This will allow you to compare how Louis saw himself with how others saw him. Second, evidence has been chosen which illuminates the various debates reviewed in Section C. No selection of sources can avoid excluding many others; but I hope always to have opened up questions and issues without assuming any answers.

Now a word about the versions of documents which have been used. The vast majority of the extracts were originally written in French. Reliable English translations of some already exist; but quite a few appear in English for the first time here. However, I decided to consult the original French editions in all cases, and then to make my own translations. This has the advantage of ensuring that French terms are rendered consistently throughout. The intentions of earlier translators varied considerably – from the heavily literal to the remarkably free – and it therefore seemed preferable to offer a more uniform treatment of all extracts. In the case of those documents originally composed in English, I have modernised spelling and punctuation, but retained the original vocabulary. Where necessary, notes have been added to explain obscure words and phrases.

Two other technical points require brief explanation: the calendar and the currency. All dates in this book have been given in the Gregorian Calendar, the system adopted by France in 1582 and still used throughout Europe today. Until 1752, Great Britain followed the Julian Calendar, which was eleven days behind the Gregorian. For example, the date of Louis XIV's death was 1 September 1715 according to the calendar used in France, but 22 August according to that used in Great Britain. This time-lag should be remembered when comparing contemporary British sources with the original material presented here.

Second, the system of currency used in seventeenth-century France needs elucidating. The relative values of the four most important units of coinage were as follows:

> 1 *écu* = 3 *livres*
> 1 *livre* = 20 *sous*
> 1 *sou* = 5 *centimes*

It is extremely difficult to relate these units to modern values. An average daily wage in late seventeenth-century France was 12–18 *sous* for a man and 5–7 *sous* for a woman. A meal at a typical inn would have cost between 15 and 25 *sous*. Exchange rates between European currencies varied considerably throughout this period, but £1 sterling was usually equivalent to about 15 *livres* or 5 *écus*.

The lay-out of this book is as follows. Chapter 1 explores the theme of 'absolutism' in both theory and practice. Then follow four parallel chapters devoted to, respectively, Louis's economic, social, religious and foreign policies. The sixth chapter examines the politics and culture of Louis's Court at Versailles. Finally, Chapter 7 returns to the controversies which surround Louis's career. It presents ten contrasting assessments of his personality, policies and achievements written by twentieth-century historians. The Bibliography contains a list of books and articles in which these various topics may be explored further.

1 Absolutism: theory and practice

Louis XIV's régime is often described as 'absolutist'. It has been argued that the King was the unique source of political authority; that he was the centre of government and the 'fountainhead' of the judicial system; and that his powers and freedom of decision were so great as to be effectively unlimited. Many historians have suggested that Louis actually achieved a commanding position of which other monarchs could only dream. He has provided the yardstick by which the powers of other European monarchs in the seventeenth century are judged. This chapter is devoted entirely to the question of whether it is fair to label Louis's rule 'absolutist'. The first section examines contemporary ideologies of royal power. We will look at Louis's own views as presented in his *Mémoires*, written during the 1660s, and in a memorandum of 1679; and then at the opinions of Bishop Bossuet, one of the leading political theorists of Louis's reign. In the second section, we will turn to the realities of royal government, and assess how far these theories were actually put into practice. Here I have chosen extracts which illuminate the working relationships between the King and his ministers, Louis's management of policy, and the nature of royal intervention in the provinces. We will explore how energetically Louis sought to impose his will, what obstacles he faced, and how successfully he overcame them.

The theory

This section begins with three excerpts from Louis's *Mémoires* which discuss the office of king, and the powers and responsibilities which it carried. These *Mémoires* were written 'for the instruction of the Dauphin' (the King's eldest son and heir to the French throne). They were drafted in the late 1660s by a team of secretaries working from notes written or dictated by Louis. The King then carefully corrected these drafts himself, often rewriting whole passages, and the *Mémoires* are thus an accurate record of his own beliefs. In the first extract [1.1], Louis explains the need for a king to become almost omniscient, and at all times to supervise and control the activities of his advisers and servants:

1.1

The function of kings . . . is to . . . observe the whole earth, to learn the news of every province and every nation, the secrets of every court, the attitudes and weaknesses of every foreign prince and his ministers; to be informed about an infinite number of things that we are presumed not to know about, to see what our subjects carefully hide from us, to discover the most obscure ideas and the most   5
hidden interests of our courtiers . . . and I don't know, finally, what other pleasure we would not abandon for this one, for the sake of curiosity alone . . . I commanded the four Secretaries of State not to sign anything at all without talking to me about it, the Superintendent [of Finances][1] likewise, and no financial business to be transacted without being registered in a book, that was to remain   10
with me, with a much abridged summary, where I could always see at a glance the current balance and the expenditures made or pending. The Chancellor[2] received a similar order . . . not to seal anything without my command, except for letters of justice . . . All requests for mercies of any type had to be made directly to me, and I granted all my subjects without distinction the privilege of appealing to me at any   15
time, in person or by petitions . . . I resolved above all not to have a chief minister . . . there being nothing more shameful than to see on the one hand all the functions and on the other the mere title of king.

[1] 'the Superintendent of Finances' = Jean-Baptiste Colbert (see below).
[2] 'The Chancellor' = Pierre Séguier (1588–1672).

Mémoires de Louis XIV, ed. J. Longnon (Paris, 1927) (hereafter cited as Mémoires de Louis XIV)

This desire for extensive royal powers and oversight did not, however, imply that the king could behave irresponsibly. In 1.2, Louis indicates that he was keenly aware of his duties towards his subjects, and felt a real vocation to serve and protect them. Louis wanted to be seen as the 'father' of his people:

1.2

My son, we must consider the good of our subjects far more than our own. They are almost part of us, for we are the head of a body of which they are the members. It is only for their own advantage that we must give them laws, and we should only use this power which we have over them to work more effectively for their happiness. It is wonderful to deserve from them the name of father along with that   5
of master, and if the one belongs to us by the right of our birth, the other must be

the sweetest object of our ambition. I know that this wonderful title is not obtained without much effort, but in praiseworthy undertakings you must not be stopped by the prospect of difficulty.

Mémoires de Louis XIV

Another goal which Louis thought worth pursuing through every adversity was 'glory'. In late seventeenth-century France, 'glory' (*la gloire*) was a highly complex term which conveyed a subtle blend of fame, honour and magnanimity. Although earlier French monarchs such as Francis I (1515–47) and Henry IV (1589–1610) had some general notion of 'glory', Louis XIV developed the idea more precisely and followed it more self-consciously than any of his predecessors. It forms a theme to which we shall often return during the course of this book. In the final extract from his *Mémoires* [1.3], Louis ponders the need for a certain pragmatism if a monarch was to attain 'glory':

1.3

There are moments when, requiring only our valour in order to succeed, we do not need any other means, but there are others when prudence is the only way to achieve our goal, and it seems as if we should suspend the use of all our other virtues for its sake . . . The wisdom lies in choosing the right policy at the right time, and nothing makes the fortunes of a prince more stable and less changing . . .   5
than his ability to change his tone, his expression, his bearing, and his direction when necessary . . . The virtue does not always lie in doing the same thing, but in always aiming at the same end; and although this end, which is none other than our glory and the greatness of our state, may actually always be the same, the means to attain it, however, are not. Those who are useful at one time may often be harmful   10
at another. The world in which we live is subject to so many changes that we cannot possibly continue the same policy for long. The able monarch, just like the wise pilot, can sail with every wind, and experience has repeatedly shown two entirely opposite ways of acting perfectly reconciled by the difference in the times and both of them ultimately producing the same happy result.

Mémoires de Louis XIV

Growing pressure on his time unfortunately meant that Louis's *Mémoires* become much more patchy after 1668–9. However, in 1679 he again penned some general thoughts on the nature of kingship in a private memorandum entitled 'Reflections on the Role of King'. 1.4 is taken from the central section of this document.

1.4

Kings are often obliged to act contrary to their inclination in a way that harms their own natural good instincts. They want to give pleasure, and they often have to punish and ruin people whom they personally like. The interests of the State must come first . . . It is necessary to guard against oneself, to beware of one's own inclinations, and to be always on the watch over one's natural self. The role of king 5 is a great one, noble and pleasing when one feels oneself worthy of performing all duties well; but it is not exempt from troubles, fatigue and anxieties. Uncertainty sometimes makes one lose heart, and when one has spent a reasonable amount of time examining a problem one must reach a decision, and take the course one believes to be best. When one has the State in view, one is working for oneself. 10 The good of the one enhances the glory of the other. When the State is happy, eminent, and powerful, the architect of this is covered with glory, and as a consequence has a right to enjoy all that is most agreeable in life to a greater degree than his subjects, in proportion to his position and theirs.

Louis XIV, 'Reflections on the Role of King', in *A King's Lessons in Statecraft*, ed. J. Longnon, trans. H. Wilson (London, 1924)

Questions

1 Explain and comment on the following phrases:
   (i) 'I resolved above all not to have a chief minister' [1.1, **lines 16–17**]
   (ii) 'The interests of the State must come first' [1.4, **lines 3–4**].
2 How realistic do you find Louis's goals as outlined in 1.1–1.4?
3 Are Louis's aims in 1.1–1.4 compatible or incompatible? Give reasons for your answer.
4 How far does 'absolutism' accurately describe the sort of power which Louis is seeking in 1.1–1.4?
5 There is a story that Louis once said 'I am the State' ('l'état, c'est moi'). The truth of this is uncertain, but how plausible do you find it in the light of 1.1–1.4?
6 Does Louis acknowledge any limitations on his authority in 1.1–1.4? If so, what are they?

We now move from Louis's own views on the nature of kingship to those of one of his leading subjects. Jacques-Bénigne Bossuet (1627–1704) was a distinguished theologian, political theorist and Court preacher. He was appointed tutor to the Dauphin in 1670. It was while he held this office that he composed the *Politics drawn from the true words of Holy Scripture*, from which the next three extracts [1.5–1.7] are all taken. 1.5 comes from the start of Book Three, in which Bossuet 'begins to explain the nature and the properties of royal authority':

1.5

Royal authority is sacred . . . God established kings as his ministers, and reigns through them over the nations . . . All power comes from God . . . Princes therefore act as ministers of God, and his lieutenants on earth. It is through them that he exercises his rule . . . The royal throne is not the throne of a man, but the throne of God himself . . . It appears from all this that the person of kings is   5
sacred, and that to try to harm them is a sacrilege . . . There is thus something religious in the respect which one owes to a prince.

Jacques-Bénigne Bossuet, *Politique tirée des propres paroles de l'Ecriture Sainte*, ed. J. Le Brun (Geneva, 1967) (hereafter cited as Bossuet, *Politique*)

However, Bossuet then went on to argue that precisely because their powers came from God, kings were obliged to use them responsibly:

1.6

Kings must respect their own power, and only use it for the public good. Their power coming from on high . . . they must not believe that they are masters of it to use it according to their own will; but they must use it with fear and restraint, as something which comes to them from God, and for which God will call them to account . . . Kings should therefore tremble in employing the power which God   5
gives them, and imagine how horrible is the sacrilege of abusing a power which comes from God. We have seen kings sitting on the throne of the Lord, holding the sword which he has himself placed in their hand. What profanation and what audacity of unjust kings, to sit on the throne of God and then give judgements contrary to his laws, and to use the sword which he puts in their hand to perpetrate   10
atrocities and to slaughter his children! Let them therefore respect their power, for it is not their power, but the power of God, which must be used piously and religiously . . . Let them rule as God rules, in a manner noble, disinterested, beneficent, in a word, divine . . . It follows from all this that the name of king is a name for father, and that goodness is the most natural characteristic of kings . . .   15
The prince is not born for himself but for the public, [and] . . . must provide for the needs of the people.

Bossuet, *Politique*

Bossuet then describes in detail the various 'characteristics of royalty'. His account culminates in a fundamental distinction between 'absolute government' and 'arbitrary government':

1.7

Royal authority is absolute. In order to make this term odious and intolerable, some pretend to confuse absolute government and arbitrary government. But there is nothing more different . . . Arbitrary government [is characterised by] four conditions. Firstly: the subjects are born slaves, that is to say truly serfs; and among them there are no free people. Secondly: nobody possesses any property: all funds belong to the prince, and there is no right of inheritance, not even from father to son. Thirdly: the prince has the right to arrange as he pleases, not only the goods but also the lives of his subjects, as one would do with slaves. And finally, in the fourth place: there is no law except his will . . . It is one thing for a government to be absolute, quite another for it to be arbitrary. It is absolute [because] . . . there is no power able to coerce the sovereign, who in that sense is independent of all human authority. But it does not follow from this that government is arbitrary, for besides the fact that everything is submitted to God's judgement . . . everybody remains the legitimate owner of their goods and nobody believes that their right to property will ever prejudice the laws, which are constantly vigilant against injustice and violence. And it is this which ensures legitimate government, opposed by its very nature to arbitrary government.

5

10

15

Bossuet, *Politique*

Questions

1   Explain and comment on the following phrases:
  (i)   'Royal authority is sacred' [**1.5, line 1**]
  (ii) 'Royal authority is absolute' [**1.7, line 1**].
2   Use **1.7** to summarise Bossuet's distinction between 'absolute government' and 'arbitrary government'.
3   Do **1.5–1.7** indicate that Bossuet believed in monarchy by 'divine right'? Explain your answer.
4   Is there evidence in **1.5–1.7** that Bossuet thought royal powers were limited? If so, in what ways were they limited?
5   In what ways do Bossuet's views on kingship [**1.5–1.7**] resemble those of Louis XIV [**1.1–1.4**]? In what ways are they different?
6   From the material in this chapter so far, and your wider knowledge, how far would you say there was a coherent theory of 'absolutism' in late seventeenth-century France? Explain your answer.
7   Using **1.1–1.7**, and your broader reading, would you say that a belief in monarchy by 'divine right' was the same as a belief in 'absolutism'? If not, in what ways were they different?

The practice

The second half of this chapter explores how far these theories of kingship were put into practice. Do the writings of Louis and Bossuet accurately describe how France was actually governed? Or do they merely outline a system which their authors wished to see established? We will look in turn at Louis's personal direction of business; at his relations with his ministers; and at the impact of central government on the French provinces.

The first three extracts present a pair of case studies illustrating Louis's involvement in the day-to-day processes of administration. 1.8 and 1.9 relate to the election of a new mayor of Beauvais in the summer of 1677. On 12 August Louis wrote to the town council and aldermen:

1.8

Dear and good friends: wishing that Monsieur Le Gay, former mayor of our town of Beauvais, should perform the duties of mayor of our said town during the present year, we write to tell you that notwithstanding the election which has already taken place of Monsieur de la Motte, you are to assemble again to elect the said Le Gay as mayor of our said town, in the customary way. Do not fail in this,   5
for this is our pleasure.

Louis XIV to the Council and Aldermen of Beauvais, 12 August 1677, in *Correspondance administrative sous la règne de Louis XIV*, **ed. G.B. Depping (4 vols., Paris, 1850–5) (hereafter cited as Depping), vol. I**

Monsieur Le Gay was duly elected mayor. When his term of office expired a year later, Louis wrote a second letter, dated 1 August 1678:

1.9

Because the services which Monsieur Le Gay, Mayor of our town of Beauvais, have rendered to us since his election have proved agreeable to us, we have resolved to maintain him further in the said office. We are therefore writing you this letter to inform you that our intention is that he shall continue to perform the duties of mayor for another year, and that to this end you will cast your votes for   5
him.

Louis XIV to the Council and Aldermen of Beauvais, 1 August 1678, in Depping vol. I

Once again, the councillors and aldermen elected Le Gay. 1.10 provides another illustration of Louis's personal attention to developments in the

French provinces. In December 1676 he was so impressed by the taxes voted by the Estates (representative assemblies) of Languedoc that he granted them a special rebate. He wrote to his uncle, the Duc de Verneuil, who was Governor of Languedoc:

1.10

I see from your letter to me the sum which the Estates of Languedoc have granted me, and all the circumstances which make this new sign of their loyalty agreeable to me. I am so satisfied with them that the almost infinite expenses with which I am oppressed have not prevented my giving them a remission of 300,000 *livres*[1] on the three million brought by their decision.

[1] '*livres*' = French currency, valued at 100 *centimes* each.

Louis XIV to the Duc de Verneuil, 18 December 1676, in Depping vol. I

Questions

1   Comment on the phrase 'for this is our pleasure' [1.8, line 6].
2   What reasons does Louis give in 1.8 and 1.9 for wanting Monsieur Le Gay to be elected Mayor of Beauvais?
3   Comment on the tone of 1.8–1.10.
4   What do 1.8–1.10 tell us about the nature of Louis's power and the workings of his régime?
5   To what extent do 1.8–1.10 demonstrate Louis's achievement of ideals which he expressed in 1.1–1.4?
6   How far do you think that the kind of royal intervention documented in 1.8–1.10 was typical or exceptional? Explain your answer.

Yet, inevitably, it was not possible for one person to know everything which happened in France, and to direct affairs single-handed. Louis required the help of ministers and advisers, and it is vital to determine whether their activities strengthened or weakened his own power. Did they assist the King by keeping him fully informed; or did they limit his freedom of action by taking decisions themselves? The next five documents [1.11–1.15] throw light on this question.

Perhaps the most famous of all Louis's ministers was Jean-Baptiste Colbert (1619–83), who became Superintendent of Finances in 1661 and Superintendent of Commerce in 1665. He continued to hold both offices until his death. 1.11 is taken from one of Colbert's many reports to the King, with the latter's annotations in the left-hand margin:

1.11

It must be done as soon as possible.

All the merchants are asking if it please Your Majesty to permit the circulation of Spanish royals at 3 *livres*[1] 58 *sous*,[2] at which they have been fixed by the last decree issued in Your Majesty's presence, and I believe that this is necessary.   5

Good.

The edict for the alienation of the tax on timber in the province in Normandy has been registered in the courts.

As you judge most appropriate.

I estimate that this will yield four to five million *livres*.[1] It is necessary to know if Your Majesty wants   10
it to be farmed out at a discount of one-sixth, or whether it should be collected direct. Farming is more secure, and the tax farmers are more determined than the commissioners who would have to be established; but perhaps, by direct collection,   15
one could save something on the discount.

It is for you to judge which is best.

My advice would be to farm it out; I will await Your Majesty's order.

The ordinances are signed.

I ask you to sign the enclosed ordinances.

I will be very happy to have news of Versailles.

I am setting off for Versailles; I will report to Your   20
Majesty tomorrow about the state of the building works.

[1] '*livres*': see 1.10, note 1.
[2] '*sous*' = French currency, valued at five *centimes* each.

Colbert to Louis XIV, 24 May 1673, in *Lettres, instructions et mémoires de Colbert*, ed. P. Clément (7 vols., Paris, 1861–82) (hereafter cited as Clément), vol. II (i)

But the working relationship between the King and his Superintendent of Finances was not always quite so harmonious. On 24 April 1671 we find Louis writing to Colbert:

1.12

I was sufficiently master of myself, the day before yesterday, to hide from you the pain which I felt on hearing someone like you, on whom I have heaped kindnesses, speak to me as you did. I have felt much friendship for you, as is clear from my actions; I still feel this, and I believe I give you firm evidence of it when I tell you that I restrained myself for your sake, and that I did not wish to say to your face   5
what I am now writing in case you displease me further. It is the memory of the services which you have given me, together with my friendship, which make me give this advice: profit from it and do not risk angering me again, for, after I have

listened to your opinions and those of your colleagues, and have pronounced on all your statements, I never wish to hear the subject mentioned again . . . I do not   10 want a single complaint. I am telling you what I think so that you can work on a secure basis and will not take any more wrong steps.

Louis XIV to Colbert, 24 April 1671, in *Collection de documents inédits sur l'histoire de France,* **ed. M. Champollion Figeac (4 vols., Paris, 1841–8) (hereafter cited as Champollion Figeac), vol. II**

However, two days later the King again wrote to Colbert:

1.13

Do not think that my friendship is diminishing: that cannot happen as long as your services continue; but I must direct them as I wish, and believe that everything I do is for the best. The preference which you fear I give to others must not offend you. My only wish is not to commit injustice and to work for the good of my people. This is what I shall do when you are near me. In the meantime, believe that I am   5 unchanged towards you, and that my feelings are all you would wish.

Louis XIV to Colbert, 26 April 1671, in Champollion Figeac vol. II

This sequence of documents concludes with two different assessments of Louis's relations with his ministers, both written by contemporaries who spent much time at Louis's Court. **1.14** was written in the 1670s by Jean-Baptiste Primi Visconti, an accomplished writer, political commentator and courtier. Visconti wrote on many subjects, including international diplomacy and the occult, but he is best known for his *Memoirs on the Court of Louis XIV*. By contrast, **1.15** is taken from the memoirs of one of the most articulate (but also most hostile) observers of the Court, the Duc de Saint-Simon (1675–1755). It was written in 1715, shortly after Louis's death.

1.14

The King does all he can to prove he is not in the least dominated by his ministers, and no prince has ever been less governed. He wishes to know everything: from his ministers, about State affairs . . . in short, during a day few things take place of which he is not informed, and there are few people whose name and habits he does not know. He has an observant eye, knows the innermost secret of each person,   5 and once he has seen a man or heard talk about him, he never forgets him.

Jean-Baptiste Primi Visconti, *Mémoires sur la cour de Louis XIV,* **ed. J. Lemoine (Paris, 1908)**

1.15

[Louis XIV] wished to reign by himself; his constant jealousy on this matter amounted to a weakness. He genuinely reigned in small matters; the big he could not attain, and even in the small he was often influenced . . . Colbert completely controlled the finances, but made Louis believe that everything passed through his hands by overwhelming him with documents for his signature . . . The superior 5
ability of his early ministers and his early generals soon wearied him. Thus he chose his ministers, not for their knowledge, but for their ignorance; not for their capacity, but for their lack of it. He liked to mould them, as he said; liked to teach them even the most trifling things . . . Those whom he favoured owed his affection for them to their endless flatteries. This is what gave his ministers so much 10
authority, through the constant opportunities which they had to praise him, to attribute everything to him, and to pretend to have learnt everything from him.

Mémoires de Saint-Simon, ed. A. de Boislisle (41 vols., Paris, 1879–1928) (hereafter cited as *Mémoires de Saint-Simon*), vol. XXVIII

Questions

1 What may be gleaned from 1.11–1.13 about the relationship between Louis XIV and Colbert?

2 What do 1.11–1.13 reveal about Louis XIV's expectations of his chief ministers?

3 What do 1.11–1.13 reveal about Colbert's suitability to be one of Louis XIV's chief ministers?

4 Do 1.11–1.13 show Louis practising the ideals which he expressed in 1.1? Give reasons for your answer.

5 Do 1.14 and 1.15 share a common view of Louis XIV's relations with his ministers? If so, what is it? If not, what do they disagree about?

6 Do the dates at which 1.14 and 1.15 were written help to explain their contents? Give reasons for your answer.

7 From the evidence in 1.11–1.13, are you more persuaded by Visconti [1.14] or by Saint-Simon [1.15]? Explain your response.

8 Using the evidence elsewhere in this book, and your wider knowledge, consider how far Louis's relations with Colbert resembled those with other leading ministers.

With the last group of extracts [1.16–1.18] we move away from the centre into the provinces. How well informed was the government about what happened in the country at large? How far was Louis able to make himself obeyed outside Paris? Perhaps the most important agents of central government in the localities were the *intendants*. These officials were appointed to each town or region, and were deliberately selected from outside the area which they controlled. The annual instructions sent to them from Paris indicate the nature and extent of their powers. 1.16 is taken from Colbert's instructions to all *intendants* in June 1680:

1.16

The King instructs me to repeat strongly to you the orders which His Majesty has given you in all previous years about the inspection of the generality [= district] in which you serve. He wants you to apply yourself with even more determination to this inspection than you have done in previous years because he wants equality and justice in allocation of taxes, and a reduction in all sorts of abuses and expenses, to   5 provide further relief for his people, beyond that which the tax reduction gives them. His Majesty therefore wishes that as soon as you receive this letter, you should begin your visit of each of the *élections*[1] in your generality; that . . . you should examine carefully the extent of landed wealth, the quality of livestock, the manufactures and everything in each *élection* which helps to attract money   10 there . . . You must also examine in each *élection* the state of tax collection, both for the past year and the present, give all necessary orders to encourage it, and search for means . . . to regulate the collection . . . His Majesty also wants you . . . to make sure that there are no mints making false coins; and, if you do find one, to send word about it at once, so that His Majesty can give the necessary orders for   15 bringing the culprits to justice immediately, there being no crime more prejudicial to his subjects than this.

[1] '*élections*' = administrative sub-divisions within each generality, originally devised for the purposes of taxation.

Colbert to all *intendants*, 1 June 1680, in Clément vol. II (i)

The *intendants* acted as the government's eyes and ears throughout France. They were Louis's troubleshooters in the localities, and their powers expanded considerably during his reign. Equally, the King and his ministers kept the *intendants* under very close observation, and reprimanded them if they overstepped their authority. In December 1672, for example, Colbert wrote to the *intendant* of Rouen:

1.17

You must not reject . . . the advice which His Majesty has instructed me to give you about your conduct, for the King acts with a profound and complete knowledge which cannot be deceived . . . I believe I have already warned you to

take cognisance only of matters which are within your competence . . . Take care
to remain within the limits of the powers which are given to you by the decisions of 5
the council.

**Colbert to Monsieur de Creil, *intendant* of Rouen, 3 February 1673, in
Clément vol. II (i)**

The government could only work effectively through its local officials if it
had reliable, up-to-date information about what was happening up and
down France. The sheer range of knowledge which this required is
indicated by an extract from Colbert's instructions in September 1663 for
the first ever general survey of France [1.18]. Special commissioners were
sent out into the provinces to gain detailed information which could then
be used to plan all sorts of policies – financial, industrial, military, judicial,
ecclesiastical:

1.18

[The commissioners] are to compile true accounts of everything of which the King
wishes to be informed, viz.: Ecclesiastical: as regards the Church, the name and
number of the bishops; the cities, towns, villages and parishes which are under
their ecclesiastical jurisdiction, their temporal holdings and the towns and parishes
of which they are composed; particularly if the bishop is temporal lord of the   5
cathedral city; the name, age, estate and temperament of the bishop, whether he is
from the region or not, whether he usually resides there . . . Military: . . . begin
with the nobility designated as governors-general, their ancestry and family ties in
the province; if they currently reside there; their good and bad conduct; if they are
accused of taking money or of vexing the people in any other way, if the   10
accusations are plausible . . . Financial: . . . it will be good to know the names of
the officials . . . if there is any manifest corruption among them; if anyone has
caused a stir, find out about it in detail; . . . if the people complain about any
vexation on their part.

**Colbert to the commissioners for a general survey of France, September
1663, in Clément vol. IV**

Questions

1 Explain and comment on the statement that 'the King acts with a
  profound and complete knowledge' [1.17, lines 2–3].

2 What may be learnt from 1.16 and 1.17 about the strengths and
  weaknesses of the system of *intendants*?

3 What does 1.18 tell you about the nature and objectives of Louis XIV's régime?

4 Use 1.8–1.18 to outline the obstacles which faced the creation of an 'absolutist' régime in late seventeenth-century France.

5 From the evidence presented in this chapter as a whole, how successful do you think Louis XIV was in the achievement of his aims? Explain your answer.

6 To what extent were the theories and practices examined in this chapter dependent on Louis's individual personality? Could they have continued under a different monarch? Discuss the implications of your answer.

7 Comment on the following two assessments of Louis XIV's régime:
   (i) 'In both theory and practice, Louis XIV's rule marked the apotheosis of absolutism'
   (ii) 'Louis XIV's wishes were constantly modified or thwarted by ministers, local officials and problems of distance'.

8 If you conclude that Louis XIV's system of government was not 'absolutist', then how would you describe it? Explain your answer.

2 Economic policies

In this chapter we turn to the economic and financial policies pursued during the reign of Louis XIV. But first we should remember that the term 'policy' may be anachronistic when applied to late seventeenth-century France. The concept of a 'planned economy', in which coherent policies and priorities are designed for the whole economic system, is very much a twentieth-century one. It was unthinkable before the industrial and technological revolutions, in societies which relied heavily upon agriculture, and where harvest failure meant widespread poverty and starvation. These basic constraints inevitably reduced the options open to Louis, and in turn limit the questions which modern historians can ask.

Nevertheless, the surviving evidence for Louis XIV's France raises a number of important issues. How did the King wish to organise his financial affairs? How far was the government able to measure and control economic trends? To what extent, and by what means, was it possible to stimulate industrial and commercial growth? And can we determine whether France became more or less prosperous during Louis's reign? The extracts which follow are drawn from a combination of official and unofficial sources, so that you can weigh up the views of the government against the observations of private individuals.

Once again, we begin with Louis's own reflections. Perhaps the most powerful minister in France during the first eighteen months of Louis's personal rule was Nicolas Fouquet (1615–80), the Superintendent of Finances. With his vast palaces at Vaux-le-Vicomte and Belle-Ile, Fouquet may even have wished to emulate Cardinal Mazarin. But in September 1661, on Louis's orders, Fouquet was arrested and disgraced. In 2.1, Louis explains his motives, and then outlines the importance which he attached to personal control of financial administration.

2.1

I realised that I should give serious attention to financial recovery, and the first thing which I judged necessary was the removal from their positions of the principal officials who had caused chaos. For ever since I took control of my affairs, I had daily uncovered new evidence of their wastefulness, and especially by the Superintendent [of Finances].[1] The sight of the vast establishments which this 5 man had designed, and the insolent acquisitions which he had made, could not but convince me of his wild ambition, and the general distress of my subjects constantly demanded that I bring him to justice . . . It must be added that of all the royal duties, the one which the prince must guard most jealously is the management of the finances. It is the most delicate of all, for it is the one most 10 capable of seducing those who perform it, and the one which makes it easiest to corrupt others. The prince alone must have the sovereign direction of it, because he alone has no fortune to create except that of the state, no acquisition to make except for the extension of the monarchy, no authority to strengthen except that of the laws, no debts to pay except the public charges, no friend to enrich except his 15 subjects.

[1] 'Superintendent [of Finances]' = Fouquet.

Mémoires de Louis XIV

In a second extract from his *Mémoires* [2.2], Louis develops these points and explains why success in all sorts of matters ultimately depended upon sound financial management:

2.2

[A king's] plans must be more varied, more extensive and more hidden than those of any private individual, of such a nature . . . that sometimes there is scarcely a single person in the world to whom he can confide them completely. There are however none of these plans into which finances do not enter somewhere. But it goes deeper than that: there is no project which does not depend absolutely and 5 essentially upon them, for what is great and beautiful when our financial circumstances allow becomes illusory and ridiculous when they do not. Think then, I beg you, how a king could govern and not be governed, if, having neglected these financial details, his best and noblest thoughts are subject to the whim of his chief minister, or the Superintendent [of Finances], or the treasurer, or of some 10 obscure and unknown clerk, whom he would be obliged to consult like so many oracles, so that he could not undertake anything except with their permission and their support.

Mémoires de Louis XIV

Questions

1   Use **2.1–2.2** to summarise the reasons why Louis XIV thought financial management important.

2   How convincing do you find the reasons which Louis gives in **2.1** for the arrest of Fouquet? What other motives may he have had?

3   How realistic do you find the aims expressed in **2.2**? Justify your response.

4   'Financial absolutism'. Is this an accurate description of Louis's aims as presented in **2.1–2.2**? Explain your answer.

5   Do you agree with Louis's emphasis on the importance of financial management [**2.1–2.2**], or do you find it exaggerated in the light of evidence elsewhere in this book, and your wider knowledge of the period?

We must now consider the extent to which these ideas were actually put into practice. When Louis assumed personal control of French government in March 1661, one of his first priorities was to prevent officials from abusing their powers and to root out corruption. **2.3** is taken from his edict of November 1661, which established a 'Chamber of Justice to investigate abuses and malpractices in the finances since 1635':

2.3

We have deemed that there could be no more just task, nor a better response to the many favours which heaven has granted us and our State, than to make our subjects feel once again the effects of peace and public tranquillity . . . This is why we have decided to take over the care and direction of [the finances] ourself, and to study in detail all the receipts and expenses of our kingdom, believing that there is   5 no other means so effective for re-establishing order and preventing waste: and we have recognised that the disorders and malpractices which have been committed for several years in the running of our finances have produced all the evils which our people have suffered, and have caused the extraordinary taxes which have had to be imposed on them in order to meet the pressing needs of the State . . . We   10 have therefore resolved . . . to impose exemplary and severe punishments on all those accused of embezzlement in our finances . . . To this end . . . we have set up and established a Chamber of Justice composed of officers from our sovereign courts.[1]

[1] 'sovereign courts' = courts which claimed that their judgements were without right of appeal.

Royal edict, November 1661, in Clément vol. II (ii)

This government supervision of financial affairs was not confined to the prevention of corruption. It also involved a detailed monitoring of the King's finances, and minute calculations of his receipts and expenditure for each year. Colbert's annual summaries of royal finances – such as that for the year 1680 [2.4] – were presented in a condensed form which could fit into the King's pocket. All sums are given in *livres*, which were worth one hundred *centimes* each.

2.4

Receipts

1	Tax farms[1]	29,318,762
2	*Recettes générales*[2]	23,894,659
3	*Recettes générales* and free gifts from *pays d'états*[3]	7,369,411
4	Woods and forests[4]	865,736
5	Extraordinary sums[5]	13,961,374
6	Anticipation of receipts for the year 1681	16,349,414
	Total receipts for the year 1680	91,759,356

Expenditure

The King's household	763,338
Victualling [= food and drink] account	1,917,413
Extraordinary household expenses	2,246,803
Butchery account	398,510
Royal mews	817,489
Purchase of horses	12,000
Treasurer of the Offertory	88,437
Justice of the Household	61,050
Royal Guard	187,335
Swiss Guard [= inner royal guard of 100 Swiss]	69,303
Hunting and falconry	342,044
Wolf hunting	34,293
The Queen's household	1,381,128
Madame la Dauphine's household	867,498
Monsieur's [= the King's brother's] household	1,198,000
Madame's household	252,000
Favours and rewards	193,336

Ready cash for the King's personal use	2,030,092
Building and maintenance of royal houses	8,513,804
Swiss Regiment	262,000
Garrisons	2,345,269
Military supplies	1,509,502
Bread ration	86,571
Extraordinary military expenses	31,233,986
Bounties to commanders of troops	825,616
Navy	4,928,773
Galleys[6]	2,869,223
Fortifications	4,603,386
Embassies	810,100
The Bastille [= the main royal prison in Paris]	189,330
Salaries	1,215,700
Emoluments of officials	2,302,427
Emoluments of marshals of France	276,150
Ordonnances de comptant[7] for rewards	2,176,988
Ordonnances de comptant for secret business	2,224,969
Other emoluments	491,400
Roads and bridges	300,364
Paving of Paris	58,258
Payment of back-interest on government bonds	1,182,013
Reimbursements	10,792,927
Commerce	324,281
Interest on loans and expenses of tax collection	2,389,200
Small gifts paid by ordinance	784,813
Travel	406,892
Total expenditure	95,964,011
Deficit for the year 1680	4,204,655

[1] 'Tax farms': profits from certain taxes were 'farmed' out to individuals in return for fixed sums paid to the government (see document 2.12).

[2] '*Recettes générales*' = direct taxes raised without consultation in the provinces known as the *pays d'élections* (see Chapter 3).

[3] '*pays d'états*' = those provinces where representative Estates retained the right to negotiate the amount of taxes paid (see Chapter 3).

[4] 'Woods and forests': Louis received certain feudal dues from woods and forests originally leased from the Crown.

[5] 'Extraordinary sums': this category comprised a variety of miscellaneous debts and investments.

[6] 'Galleys' = long, low boats rowed by convicts.

[7] '*Ordonnances de comptant*' = orders sent to the Treasury authorising payments in cash.

Colbert's summary of the King's finances for the year 1680, in Clément vol. II (ii)

Such records of annual receipts and expenditure enabled the government to chart economic trends from year to year, and whether the King's finances were in surplus or deficit. Colbert appended to his summary a table of the King's financial situation between 1662 and 1680 [2.5]. Again, all sums are given in *livres*.

2.5

Year	Receipts	Expenditure	Surplus	Deficit
1662	75,568,750	74,826,456	742,294	
1663	48,053,826	46,826,576	1,227,250	
1664	63,602,796	63,071,008	531,788	
1665	90,883,973	90,871,856	12,117	
1666	67,459,001	66,611,895	847,106	
1667	72,520,925	72,090,744	430,181	
1668	70,875,374	70,875,381		7
1669	76,468,755	76,283,149	185,606	
1670	73,900,755	77,209,879		3,309,124
1671	87,501,077	83,875,723	3,625,354	
1672	87,067,787	87,928,561		860,774
1673	96,971,302	98,242,773		1,271,471
1674	105,738,044	106,803,861		1,065,817
1675	112,133,054	111,866,488	266,566	
1676	110,936,796	110,132,622	804,174	
1677	116,315,294	115,819,462	495,832	
1678	106,705,242	106,910,519		205,277
1679	126,132,816	128,235,300		2,102,484
1680	91,759,356	95,964,011		4,204,655

Colbert's summary of the King's finances from 1662 to 1680, in Clément vol. II (ii)

However, during the second half of Louis's reign the budget moved further and further into the red. By 1714, the King's receipts totalled 199,175,671 *livres* while his expenditure had soared to 427,119,260 *livres*, leaving a deficit of 227,943,589 *livres*. This debt was caused mainly by a series of expensive wars (see Chapter 5), and necessitated ever greater demands on the French taxpayer. The scale of these demands, and the resentment which they aroused, will become clear in documents 2.13–2.17, below.

Questions

1   Explain and comment on the following items of expenditure in 2.4:
    (i)   'Extraordinary household expenses'
    (ii)   'Favours and rewards'
    (iii) 'Building and maintenance of royal houses'
    (iv)   'Extraordinary military supplies'
    (v)   'Reimbursements'.

2   Does 2.4 suggest that Louis's financial position in 1680 was healthy? If not, in what ways was it unhealthy? Give reasons for your answer.

3   Does 2.5 indicate that the King's finances were improving or deteriorating between 1662 and 1680? Justify your response.

4   If you had been in Colbert's position in 1680, what changes (if any) would you have advised Louis to make in his financial policies, and why?

5   How far do 2.3–2.5 demonstrate the implementation of ideals expressed in 2.1–2.2? Explain your answer.

6   Comment on the usefulness to the historian of tables such as 2.4 and 2.5.

7   'Figures assembled for their own sake, with no visible influence on the government's decisions'. How far do the sources elsewhere in this book, and your wider reading, suggest that this is a fair comment on 2.4–2.5?

But for France's economy to expand and prosper in the longer term, it was not enough simply to try to balance the books. Ways had to be found to generate new wealth. The seventeenth-century French economy remained heavily dependent upon agricultural production: over 70 per cent of the population lived and worked on the land, often practising methods which had barely changed for centuries. As we shall see (document 2.14), harvest failure could bring many to the brink of starvation. Yet this period saw no significant increase in agrarian productivity: throughout Louis's reign, normal grain harvests yielded an average of three to six times the amount of seed sown. Thus the largest sector of France's economy also remained one of the most stagnant.

In their search for sustained economic growth, Louis and Colbert therefore looked beyond agriculture to the development of trade and industry. The next sequence of documents [2.6–2.8] all relate to the controversial question of commerce. Two issues were particularly contentious: first, how commerce might be encouraged; and second, the extent to which the government should regulate the activities of individual merchants in order to achieve this. Colbert devoted an immense amount of time to the development of French commerce, and was the driving force behind the establishment of a Council of Commerce which first met on 3 August 1664. At this meeting, Colbert presented a 'memoir' [2.6] on 'the state to which commerce had been reduced' and the ways in which it might be improved:

2.6

The reasons for the bad state of commerce within the kingdom . . . are . . . in short, the lack of application of the King and his council, which has in turn caused that of the lesser officials, who are responsible for policing, and therefore for the maintenance and development of all manufactures . . . I believe that we will easily agree on this principle: that it is only the abundance of money in a state which   5 makes a difference to its greatness and its power . . . In addition to the advantages which will derive from more money coming into the kingdom, it is certain that, by means of the manufactures, a million people who languish in idleness will gain their livelihood; that a further considerable number will gain their livelihood on board ship and in the sea ports; that the almost infinite expansion of the number of 10 ships will likewise expand the greatness and power of the State. These, to my mind, are the ends towards which the King should direct his efforts, his goodness, and his love for his people.

Colbert's memoir on commerce, 3 August 1664, in Clément vol. II (i)

Nonetheless, such attempts to encourage commercial growth faced formidable obstacles. In particular, the vested interests of individual merchants did not always coincide with those of the nation as a whole. As one of the leading contemporary writers on commerce, Jacques Savary, complained in his book *The Complete Merchant* (*Le Parfait Négociant*), published in 1675, 'the ignorance, imprudence and ambition of merchants are common causes of failure and bankruptcy'. Two years earlier, in a bid to root out corruption, prevent bankruptcy, and ensure uniform commercial practice throughout France, Louis had issued a massive Commercial Ordinance. This laid down in intricate detail how businesses should be organised, fraudulence punished, and the extent to which towns and cities could regulate their own commercial affairs. The preamble to the ordinance [2.7] explains its rationale.

2.7

Because commerce is the source of public wealth and of the fortunes of individuals, we have for several years taken great care to make it flourish in our kingdom. This was why we created . . . several trading companies,[1] by means of which our subjects can now draw from distant lands those goods which previously they could only acquire through the intervention of other nations. This was why we 5 committed ourselves to the construction and arming of a great number of ships to advance navigation, and to employ the strength of our arms at sea and on land in order to maintain security. As these enterprises have achieved all the success which we expected of them, we have felt obliged to safeguard their future by regulations to ensure honesty among merchants rather than fraud, and to avoid the 10 obstacles which deflect them from their tasks by lengthy lawsuits, whose costs consume most of the liquid capital which they have acquired.

[1] 'several companies': the East India and West India trading companies had been founded in 1664.

Commercial Ordinance, March 1673, in *Recueil général des anciennes lois françaises depuis l'an 420 jusqu'à la révolution de 1789*, ed. F.A. Isambert *et al.* (29 vols., Paris, 1822–33) (hereafter cited as Isambert), vol. XIX

There followed a series of immensely detailed regulations which ranged from the organisation of apprentices to the keeping of accounts, and from insolvency and bankruptcy to the jurisdiction of commercial courts. However, there were many who thought that such government restrictions violated the basic freedom of individual merchants. Some also felt that rules and regulations would ultimately prove counter-productive and decrease the volume of French commerce. In response to growing pressure from merchants that the government listen to their opinions, Louis set up a second Council of Commerce in 1700. This contained representatives of merchants throughout France, and provided a forum in which they could campaign for the removal of regulations and restrictions. 2.8 is taken from a speech delivered on 4 March 1701 by Joachim Descazeaux du Hallay, who represented the town of Nantes on the Council of Commerce.

2.8

The first thing which one can wish for to encourage commerce is liberty . . .
Liberty is the soul and element of commerce; it stimulates the minds and the industry of merchants, who, always thinking of new ways to make discoveries and enterprises, engage in ceaseless trade which produces abundance everywhere.
Once we limit the enterprise of merchants by restrictions, we destroy commerce. 5
The Dutch, whom we can cite as an example in commerce, have made a law which

they observe regularly to ensure that complete liberty reigns there. It is by this device that they have made themselves masters of the world's trade. We even see them go as far as to permit the free exit of gold and silver specie, which other nations prohibit so severely. Clever merchants know that, by an inevitable process, 10 what leaves will return by another route, and that if this cycle is properly followed it will produce a profit which will enrich the country which created it.

Speech by Joachim Descazeaux du Hallay to the Council of Commerce, 4 March 1701, in *Correspondance des contrôleurs généraux des finances,* **ed. A.M. de Boislisle (3 vols., Paris, 1874–97), vol. II**

Questions

1 Explain and comment on the following phrases:
  (i) 'it is only the abundance of money in a state which makes a difference to its greatness and its power' [2.6, lines 5–6]
  (ii) 'commerce is the source of public wealth and of the fortunes of individuals' [2.7, lines 1–2]
  (iii) 'Liberty is the soul and element of commerce' [2.8, line 2].
2 Use 2.6 and 2.7 to summarise the case for regulation of commercial activities.
3 Use 2.8 to summarise the case against regulation of commercial activities.
4 Do 2.7 and 2.8 suggest to you that the complaints expressed in 2.8 were just? Explain your answer.
5 What evidence have you found in this book, and elsewhere, that measures such as 2.6–2.7 had the desired effect? Explore the significance of your answer.

It was not only in the field of commerce that the government sought to regulate economic activity. Louis XIV's reign was also notable for a series of attempts to stimulate French industrial growth. The intricacy and thoroughness of the government's requirements are apparent in some of the instructions 'about the implementation of the general regulations for manufactures', issued on 13 August 1669 [2.9]. These instructions were to be enforced by an 'inspector-general of manufactures'.

2.9

. . . 4   [The] royal inspector shall find out whether there is a craft guild in the town where industries are established, and whether the master craftsmen have written their names on the register kept by the town clerk, and on those of the civil court and the craft guild . . . And until this is done they shall be forbidden to practise their craft, and those whose names are not   5 on the said registers will be prevented from working as masters . . .

9 A guild chamber shall be established in the town hall, if there is one, [and] if not, in the most convenient place for holding the meetings needed to transact the business of the community, and for the councillors in charge to see, inspect and mark the merchandise brought there on certain days at 10 appointed times by the craftsmen and workers . . .

15 The councillors shall as soon as possible make a general tour of all the workshops to see that their goods conform with the regulations on size . . .

16 The said councillors must also make a general tour each month of the homes of all workmen and craftsmen . . .

Instructions about the implementation of general regulations for manufactures, 13 August 1669, in Clément vol. II (ii)

In addition to these general instructions, there were also numerous occasions when Louis or Colbert personally intervened to correct some specific problem in manufacturing industries. For example, on 12 September 1670, Colbert wrote to Monsieur Barillon, the *intendant* of Amiens:

2.10

I am constantly receiving complaints against the mayor and aldermen of Amiens about their failure to enforce the statutes and regulations for manufactures, and about the frauds and abuses committed in that town. I beg you to rectify their behaviour and to make sure that they enforce the said statutes, regulations and decisions strictly; and if they prove refractory, to make an example of one of them   5 by suspending him and removing him from the magistrature.

Colbert to Monsieur Barillon, *intendant* of Amiens, 12 September 1670, in Depping vol. III

Another of Colbert's letters, written to Monsieur Le Blanc, the *intendant* of Rouen, on 21 October 1682 [2.11], reveals a similar concern with the precise details of specific industries and also indicates the government's attitude towards merchants.

2.11

You are sufficiently well aware of the importance of manufactures for the provinces to realise that you must neglect nothing which can increase them . . . From reports which I have received from the East India Company I have heard bitter complaints that the linens of Rouen are of neither the size nor the quality

which they should be, and that this will be very prejudicial to the province of   5
Normandy. I beg you therefore to make detailed enquiries of the principal
merchants as to what should be done to ensure the strict enforcement of the
regulations concerning linens, and to take all necessary precautions to prevent this
decline, and to restore to those linens the reputation which they used to enjoy in
the said Indies. But, in hearing the views of these merchants, I ask you to   10
remember that their opinions never tend towards the general good, but only
towards what furthers their own petty interests and particular trade, so that,
although you may derive information from them, you should avoid following their
opinions on this point.

**Colbert to Monsieur Le Blanc, *intendant* of Rouen, 21 October 1682, in
Clément vol. II (ii)**

Questions

1 Why might it have been necessary that 'councillors . . . make a general
   tour each month of the homes of all workmen and craftsmen' [2.9,
   lines 14–15]?
2 What reasons can you give for and against the regulations set out in
   2.9?
3 Comment on the relationship between trade and industry which
   emerges in 2.11.
4 Do 2.10 and 2.11 contain evidence that the regulations in 2.9, and
   others like them, proved difficult to enforce? Explain your answer.
5 Do 2.9–2.11 suggest that the complaints expressed in 2.8 might also
   have applied to manufacturing industry? Give reasons for your answer.
6 What do 2.10-2.11 tell you about the powers and functions of the
   intendants under Louis XIV? Is this consistent or inconsistent with what
   you found in Chapter 1? Give reasons for your answer.
7 'A state whose potential for commercial and industrial growth was
   suffocated by government restrictions.' Discuss this view of France
   under Louis XIV.

A further major problem which the government faced was how to tap the
expanding wealth of French commerce and industry. How could it raise
taxes without these in turn becoming a disincentive to economic enterprise? The French revenue system had evolved over several centuries and
by the reign of Louis XIV was extremely complex. One of the clearest
accounts of how it worked was that written by the English philosopher and

political theorist John Locke, who travelled extensively in France during the late 1670s. Locke described the system in April 1677 as follows:

2.12

There are four branches of the revenue in France: *la gabelle, les entres, les aides* [and] *la taille. Les entres* are the same [as] our customs, i.e. a tax on merchandise in motion. *Les aides* are excise on wine sold in *caberets* [= taverns] and, as I think, retail of tobacco, tin and perhaps other commodities. *La gabelle* is a tax on salt. These together are farmed at fifty millions per annum and the *taille* yields as much 5 more. The *taille* is something like a land tax, but it is laid at the King's pleasure who every year takes as much as he thinks fit. The sum being agreed on in the Council, the share of each province is sent to the respective *intendant* and there proportioned to each *généralité* [= district] its share, and so to each parish where the consuls make writ. Where anyone find himself overcharged, he has recourse to 10 the commissioners to that purpose. *Terre noble* [= noble land] pays no *taille* anywhere in the owner's hand, but if it be let, the renter pays it. In some parts land of a nobleman, whether noble or not, pays nothing, but in other parts their noble land only is excepted, but the other pays.

Locke's Travels in France, ed. John Lough (Cambridge, 1953) (hereafter cited as *Locke's Travels*)

But the burdens which this revenue system imposed on the French people were very considerable. They became even worse in wartime. In **2.13**, Locke describes the situation at the city of Tours in May 1677.

2.13

They gave the King this year 45,000 *livres*[1] to be excused from winter quarter, which came to 1/10 of the rent of their houses. Wine, wood, etc. that enter the town pay tax to the King. Besides he sends to the several companies of tradesmen for so much money as he thinks fit. The officers of each *corps de métier* [= guild] tax everyone according to his worth, which perhaps amounts to about one *écu*[2] or 5 four *livres* to a man counted worth one hundred *écus*. But a *bourgeois* [= town dweller] or tradesman that lives in the town, if he have land in the country, if he keep it in his hand or set it to rent, which is the common way, that pays nothing; but the peasant who rents it, if he be worth anything, pays for what he has, but he makes no default of his rent, for the manner of taxing in this country is this. The 10 tax to be paid being laid upon the parish, the collectors for that year assess everyone of the inhabitants or housekeepers [= householders] of the parish, according to his proportion as they judge him worth, but consider not the land in the parish that belongs to anyone living out of it. This makes them say that the

taille in France is personal . . . This is what so grinds the peasant in France. There 15
lies an appeal for the overtaxed, but I find not that the remedy is made much use
of.

¹ '*livres*' = French currency, valued at 100 *centimes* each.
² '*écu*' = a French coin, valued at three *livres*, or sixty *sous*.

Locke's Travels

These problems became dramatically worse whenever the harvest failed, as
it did, for example, in 1674. The following year the Governor of Dauphiné,
the Duc de Lesdiguières, told Colbert just how bad conditions were in
some rural areas:

2.14

I can no longer put off telling you about the misery to which I have seen this
province reduced. Commerce has completely ceased there, and from all directions
people come to me begging me to tell the King that it is impossible for them to pay
their dues. This is assuredly true, Monsieur, and I must tell you so that you are
properly informed of the situation, that the majority of the population of this   5
province lived throughout the winter only on bread made from acorns and roots,
and that at present they can be seen eating grass from the fields and the bark of
trees. I feel I am obliged to tell you of things as they really are, so as to give . . .
orders which will please His Majesty.

**The Duc de Lesdiguières, Governor of Dauphiné, to Colbert, 29 May 1675,
in Depping vol. III**

But this misery did not necessarily incline people to rebellion. Indeed,
many apparently believed that once the King knew about their plight he
would take steps to alleviate it. There is evidence to suggest that this was
not an entirely unrealistic hope. For example, on 18 February 1662, Louis
wrote as follows to the Maréchal de la Meilleraye, Governor of Brittany:

2.15

I have given orders for the purchasing in Brittany of 1,000 tons of grain and for
transporting them here [= Paris] as soon as possible, just as I have had it brought
from foreign countries and from other provinces of my kingdom where the harvest
has been better, in order to remedy the famine which has been great in these parts.
And as this is something very close to my heart, I very much wanted to write this   5
letter to you in my own hand, to let you know that I wish you to facilitate the
purchase and transport of the said quantity of grain, by doing everything which

your office authorises you to do, assisting and protecting those appointed to work on my behalf there, and completely removing any obstacles which they might encounter in the execution of my will, since the relief of my subjects is at stake.

Louis XIV to the Maréchal de la Meilleraye, 18 February 1662, in *Oeuvres de Louis XIV*, ed. M. Grouvelle (6 vols., Paris, 1806), vol. V

Another example of the government's willingness to respond to public protest may be found in the despatches of William Perwich, who was English Agent in Paris between 1669 and 1677. France was at war with Holland from 1672 to 1678, and a series of new taxes were devised in order to finance the military campaigns. Perwich's despatch of 30 August 1673 [2.16] describes some of these taxes, and public attitudes towards them.

2.16

As for this place [= Paris], the people begin to complain extremely about the new taxes; that upon paper . . . has been rejected in the provincial Parliaments, and now it is believed the weight of it shall be taken off of particular persons . . . and imposed on all in general whatever paper shall be used, wherein I shall be somewhat concerned according to the despatches I am obliged to make every day.   5
There being a great imposition laid on all the periwig makers, a tumultuous body of four hundred of their wives has been to demand misericorde [= mercy] of Monsieur Colbert, whereupon their shops are suffered to be opened again.

The Despatches of William Perwich, ed. M.B. Curran (Camden Society, third series, vol. V, 1903)

But such measures were not always enough to relieve the distress caused by heavy taxation. France was again at war between 1688 and 1697 (see Chapter 5, below), and the financial burdens on the nation as a whole became ever greater. One of those who complained most forcefully was François de Salignac de la Mothe Fénelon (1651-1715), Archbishop of Cambrai. Fénelon succeeded Bossuet as tutor to the Dauphin; but was later disgraced for refusing to condemn Madame de Guyon, an eccentric mystic whom Louis strongly disliked. Thereafter, Fénelon retired to Cambrai and quietly observed political and social developments. By the closing years of the seventeenth century he yearned to tell Louis just how much suffering his policies brought to the French people. The following letter [2.17] was probably written in the mid-1690s, but it is uncertain whether or not Fénelon ever actually sent it to the King.

2.17

Your people, whom you should love as your own children, and who have hitherto
loved you so passionately, are now dying of hunger. Cultivation of the land is
almost abandoned; the towns and the countryside are becoming depopulated; all
the trades are languishing and no longer produce workmen. All commerce is
destroyed. Thus you have drained away half the inner strength of your state in   5
order to make and defend useless conquests outside it. Instead of drawing money
from this poor people, you should give them alms and feed them. The whole of
France is no longer anything more than a great, devastated hospital, with no
provisions. The magistrates are despised and worn out. The nobility, all of whose
possessions are held by decree, live entirely on the state . . . You, Sire, have   10
brought all these troubles upon yourself; for, with the whole kingdom in ruins, you
keep everything in your own hands, and no one can live any longer except on your
gifts. This is that great kingdom which flourishes under a king who is always
depicted as the joy of his people, and who would indeed be so had flattering advice
not poisoned him! The very people (it must be said) who loved you so much, who   15
had so much confidence in you, are beginning to lose affection, trust and even
respect for you. Your victories and conquests no longer make them rejoice; they
are full of bitterness and despair . . . This, Sire, is the state that you are in.

Correspondance de Fénelon, archévêque de Cambrai, ed. A.P.P. Caron
(11 vols., Paris, 1827-9), vol. II

Questions

1   Use **2.12** to summarise the 'four branches' of French taxes.
2   Is there evidence in **2.14-2.17** that Louis XIV tried to act as the 'father'
    of his people (see document **1.2**)? Justify your response.
3   Do **2.13-2.17** share a common view of:
    (i)   the nature of France's economic problems
    (ii) the reasons for those problems?
    If so, what is it? If not, what do they disagree about?
4   Do the documents in this chapter help you to assess whether or not this
    was an absolutist régime? Explain your answer.
5   In the light of material in Chapter 2 and elsewhere, how far would you
    say Louis XIV had a coherent economic 'policy'? Explain your answer.
6   Using the evidence in this chapter, and your wider reading, answer the
    following questions, giving your reasons:
    (i)   did France become more or less prosperous under Louis XIV
    (ii) what caused it to become more or less prosperous
    (iii) how great was the King's personal control over the French
          economy?

3 Social policies

Fénelon's lament about the sufferings of the French people leads us neatly into the subject of Louis's social policies. This chapter will examine five key themes in turn: Louis's attitudes towards the nobility and the extent to which this facilitated the rise of the bourgeoisie; his management of the legal system; the role of the 'Estates' (representative assemblies) in those provinces which possessed them; the nature of social protest and revolt; and finally, as a case study in municipal administration, the regulation and government of Paris. Throughout, we must assess how far Louis's reign saw new objectives and priorities or simply the continuation of existing policies.

The early years of Louis's life were haunted by the fear of a revolt by the French nobility. The Frondes of 1648–53 (see the Introduction) marked the culmination of attempts by the nobles to reform the policies (especially financial) pursued by Louis's advisers. When he assumed personal control in 1661, Louis therefore had to treat the nobles carefully but firmly. Throughout his reign, he was very anxious to detect and punish those 'false nobles' who claimed nobility without proper title. On the other hand, Louis disliked the existing rules of *dérogéance*, whereby a noble lost his status if he engaged in a 'demeaning' occupation, such as commerce. To remedy this, in August 1669 Louis issued an 'edict permitting the nobility to participate in commerce at sea without loss of rank' [3.1].

3.1

As commerce, and particularly that by sea, is the fertile source which gives wealth to nations and spreads it to their subjects in proportion to their industry and their labour; and that there is no more blameless or lawful means of acquiring wealth; and also that it has always been held in high regard among the best ordered nations, and is universally welcomed as one of the most honourable occupations in 5 civil life; [and] although the laws and ordinances of our kingdom have quite properly forbidden the nobility to participate in retail trading, to practise the mechanical arts, and to exploit the property of others . . . we have thought it proper

to make our intention known on this subject, and to declare by a law which is to be
published and generally enforced throughout the length and breadth of our   10
kingdom, that seaborne commerce shall not cause the loss of noble rank.

**Edict permitting the nobility to participate in commerce at sea without loss
of rank, August 1669, in François Véron de Forbonnais, *Recherches et
considérations sur les finances de France* (2 vols., Basel, 1758), vol. I**

During the mid-1690s, as a further incentive to enterprise in commerce
and other fields, Louis again amended the rules governing the nobility. An
edict of March 1696 conferred 'ennoblement in return for financial
contributions upon five hundred persons chosen from amongst the most
distinguished of the realm' [3.2]. The preamble to this edict declared:

3.2

The title and the source of nobility is a gift from the prince, who knows how to
reward with discernment the important services which subjects render to their
country. These services, so worthy of a sovereign's recognition, are not always
rendered with a sword in the hand; patriotism can be shown in more than one
way . . . This is why we have resolved to grant five hundred letters of nobility in our   5
kingdom, as a reward for those of our subjects who, in acquiring them for a modest
sum, will contribute to providing the aid which we need to repel the obstinate
efforts of our enemies . . . [These] five hundred persons will be selected from
among the most distinguished in terms of merit, virtues and good qualities . . .
[They will include] even businessmen and merchants conducting wholesale trade,   10
which they will be able to continue without forfeiting the said quality of nobility . . .

Royal edict conferring ennoblement, March 1696, in Isambert vol. XX

Nor were these the only ways in which individuals could attain noble status.
Traditionally, the French nobility consisted of two groups: the ancient
nobility, or 'nobility of the sword', whose status rested upon military service
and landed wealth, and the so-called 'nobility of the robe', who derived
their titles from civil office. During his reign, Louis steadily increased the
number of offices which conferred nobility upon their occupants. A typical
example was an edict of March 1691 which reformed the offices within the
cour des aides in Paris [3.3]. This court oversaw the workings of the tax
system, heard appeals against the decisions of lower courts, and tried
criminal cases connected with taxes.

3.3

His Majesty orders the creation within the *cour des aides* in Paris of the offices of two presidents, six councillors, a third *avocat-général*[1] and two gentleman-ushers; and all the officers of the said court down to and including the first gentleman-usher shall be entitled to the status of full nobility, with all its attendant rights, privileges, honours, prerogatives, liberties and exemptions,[2] provided that they 5 have held their offices for at least twenty years, or have died while holding the said offices.

[1] *'avocat-général'* = the title given to the most senior rank of French barrister.
[2] 'exemptions': noble status carried exemption from many forms of taxation.

Royal edict reforming the *cour des aides* in Paris, 12 March 1691, in L.N.H. Chérin, *Abrégé chronologique d'édits, déclarations, règlements, arrêts et lettres patentes . . . concernant le fait de noblesse* (Paris, 1861)

However, many 'nobles of the sword' were deeply suspicious of the new categories of nobility created by Louis XIV. Their sentiments were vividly expressed by the Duc de Saint-Simon [3.4], whose father had been honoured with a duchy by Louis XIII in recognition of his ancient estates.

3.4

One might have thought that the King would have liked the great nobility, and not wished to place others on an equal footing with them. In fact, nothing could be further from the truth. The aversion which he had towards nobility of sentiment, and his weakness for his ministers, who hated and kept others down in order to raise themselves . . . had given him a similar aversion to noble birth. He feared it as 5 much as intellect, and if these two qualities were united in the same individual, and [Louis] knew it, then he would have nothing more to do with that person . . . He realised that he could intimidate a nobleman with the fear of disgrace, but he could not destroy either him or his family; whereas secretaries of state or other ministers of the same kind, whom he had promoted to their positions, could be plunged once 10 more into the oblivion from which they had been raised . . . It was for this reason that he set his ministers above even the most distinguished of his subjects . . . and never promoted a minister whom he could not destroy . . . As a result, the beautiful name of the high nobility was tarnished by a horde of riff-raff.

Mémoires de Saint-Simon, vol. XXVIII

Questions

1 Explain and comment on the following phrases:
   (i) 'the obstinate efforts of our enemies' [3.2, **lines 7–8**].
   (ii) 'the beautiful name of the high nobility was tarnished by a horde of riff-raff' [3.4, **lines 13–14**].
2 In what ways do 3.1–3.2 indicate that Louis XIV attached more importance to encouraging commerce than to preserving the status of the 'nobility of the sword'? Consider the implications of your answer.
3 Consider the motives which might have prompted a measure such as 3.3.
4 Use 3.2–3.3 to summarise the qualities and achievements necessary to become a noble in Louis XIV's France.
5 Do 3.1–3.3 reveal a coherent attitude towards the French nobility? If so, what was it? If not, in what ways are they inconsistent?
6 From the evidence in 3.1–3.3, and your wider knowledge, how fair are Saint-Simon's comments in 3.4? Explain your answer.
7 How far did Louis XIV's treatment of the nobility, as reflected in 3.1–3.4, reinforce or obstruct his policies in other areas? Give reasons for your answer.

Another field in which Louis had to tread carefully during the years after the Frondes lay in his management of the French legal system. In this period the French king's political authority was very closely related to his judicial powers, and Louis quickly realised that he could exploit his role as the ultimate source of all justice to establish control over the law courts. In his *Mémoires* he described how he handled the so-called 'sovereign courts' [3.5]. These posed a particular problem because they claimed to give judgements without any right of appeal.

3.5

It was necessary for a thousand reasons, particularly to prepare for the much needed reform of justice, to reduce the authority of the principal courts which, under the pretext that their judgements were without appeal and, as they say, sovereign . . . had gradually taken the name of 'sovereign courts', and regarded themselves as so many separate and independent sovereignties. I announced that I   5
would not tolerate their behaviour any longer. And to make an example, because the *cour des aides*[1] in Paris was the first to depart slightly from its duty, on the question of its jurisdiction, I exiled its most guilty officials, believing that a strong

dose of this remedy applied at the outset would prevent my having to use it often later; which has paid off.

[1] *'cour des aides'*: see 3.3.

Mémoires de Louis XIV

To ensure this, Louis secured a formal ruling by his Council of State to limit the jurisdiction of the 'sovereign courts' [3.6].

3.6

I made my intentions even clearer . . . by a formal decision of my supreme council. For it is very true that these courts have no power over each other, in their various jurisdictions regulated by laws and by edicts . . . I forbade them all, by this decision, from ever giving any judgements contrary to those of my council, under any pretext whatsoever, whether of their jurisdiction or of the right of individuals;   5
and I ordered them, whenever they believed that one or the other had been harmed, to complain about it to me and to have recourse to my authority, for I had entrusted them only to give justice to my subjects, and not to obtain justice for themselves, which is an aspect of sovereignty so unique to the Crown and so proper to the King alone, that it cannot be delegated to anyone else.

Mémoires de Louis XIV

By far the most troublesome of the 'sovereign courts' were the so-called *parlements*. These sat in Paris and in a number of other towns and cities, and acted as the highest courts of appeal in their respective provinces. In addition, they performed many other administrative and legal functions. Most importantly, no royal edict or declaration carried the force of law in those regions until registered by the appropriate *parlement*. Along with this went the *parlements*' right to 'remonstrate' against royal instructions. In cases of prolonged disagreement, the king could force a *parlement* to register his edicts either by direct command (*lettres de jussion*), or by holding a special ceremony of registration (a *lit de justice*). But these mechanisms, and the circumstances in which they could be used, remained highly controversial and often caused bitter resentment. This problem was compounded by the extensive jurisdictions of the *parlements*: that of the Paris *parlement* alone covered nearly one-third of France. Map **3.7** shows the provinces and *parlements* of the late seventeenth century.

3·7

The seats of the French *parlements* during the late seventeenth century

During the Frondes, many *parlements*, and especially the one in Paris, used their powers to obstruct royal policies. They provided a forum within which regional grievances could be expressed, and thus formed power-bases for provincial resistance against central authority. Several times between 1648 and 1652, the *parlements'* refusal to register edicts led to lengthy wrangles with the Crown which temporarily halted royal government in some parts of France. Yet the legal officials who composed the *parlements* (known as *parlementaires*) were quick to justify their rights and privileges. One of the most passionate and articulate defences was voiced by Omer Talon, one of the two *avocats-généraux* (see **3.3, note 1**) in the *parlement* of Paris. **3.8** is an extract from Talon's speech to that *parlement* in July 1648.

3.8

In the past, the king's wishes were never executed by his subjects without being first approved by all the great men of the kingdom, by the princes and officers of the crown. Today this political jurisdiction is vested in the *parlement*; our possession of this power is guaranteed by a long tradition and respectfully acknowledged by the people. The opposition of our votes, the respectful resistance 5 which we bring to bear in public affairs, must not be interpreted as disobedience but rather as a necessary result of the exercise of our office and of the fulfilling of our obligations, and certainly the king's majesty is not diminished by his having to respect the decrees of his kingdom; by so doing, he governs, in the words of the Scriptures, a lawful kingdom.

Omer Talon, 'Mémoires continués par Denis Talon', in *Nouvelle Collection des Mémoires relatifs à l'Histoire de France depuis le XIIIe siècle jusqu'à la fin du XVIIIe siècle*, ed. J.F. Michaud and J.J.F. Poujoulat (34 vols., Paris, 1854), vol. XXX

However, the late seventeenth century saw a gradual erosion of the *parlements'* powers. Most significantly, in April 1667 Louis XIV issued a Civil Ordinance which obliged all *parlements* 'to proceed immediately with the publication and registration of our ordinances, declarations, edicts and other letters, as soon as they shall have received them'. This was confirmed and strengthened by further instructions in August 1670 and February 1673. Yet such requirements were only enforced by constant royal vigilance. The last two documents in this sequence [**3.9–3.10**] provide two illustrations of Louis's personal intervention in the administration of justice. **3.9** is taken from his letter to the Bailiff of Etampes, dated 25 February 1671.

3.9

We are informed that . . . Julienne Morinot was condemned . . . in our town of Etampes to be executed for having starved her child to death, and recovered immediately after being hanged, and that you request a commission to rearrest her and to bring her to justice a second time. We are therefore writing to tell you that if you have received the said commission, you should postpone the execution until 5 we have issued our letters of mercy. In which you must not fail, for this is our pleasure.

Louis XIV to the Bailiff of Etampes, 25 February 1671, in Depping vol. II

In 3.10, Michel Le Tellier, who was Chancellor (head of the judicial system) from 1677, writes on Louis's behalf to the *parlement* of the province of Dauphiné, laying down the limits of the *parlement*'s jurisdiction.

3.10

The King has learnt that the *parlement* of Dauphiné has had a number of conflicts with the provost general of the province or his lieutenants, by interfering in the jurisdiction which is assigned to them by edicts and ordinances . . . Upon which matter His Majesty has commanded me to write you this letter on his behalf telling you that not only are you not entitled to receive appeals or complaints which are   5 brought to you against the decisions of the provost, or to forbid them [= the provost general . . . or his lieutenants] to continue with an action or to transfer it to your court, but also that it is not for you to judge their competence, whether it be to accord or to deprive them of the cognisance of a case.

The Chancellor Le Tellier to the *parlement* of Dauphiné at Grenoble, 9 September 1679, in Depping vol. II

Questions

1   Explain and comment on the following phrases:
   (i)   'he governs, in the words of the Scriptures, a lawful kingdom' [**3.8, lines 9–10**]
   (ii) 'our letters of mercy' [**3.9, line 6**].
2   From the evidence in **3.5–3.6**, what changes did Louis XIV seek in the French legal system? Why did he seek to do this?
3   Comment on the location of the *parlements* shown in **3.7**.
4   Do the claims advanced in **3.8** constitute a limitation on royal authority? Explain your answer.
5   'Royal absolutism was successfully extended to the legal system'. To what extent do **3.5–3.10** bear out this statement?
6   Using the material in **3.5–3.10**, and your wider knowledge, how dramatically did Louis XIV change the French legal system? Discuss the implications of your answer.
7   How far do **3.5–3.10** indicate the growth of central power at the expense of local sources of authority?

A further problem facing Louis were the Estates which met in several French provinces. These were representative assemblies which gave the French people some (very limited) influence over royal policies. Map **3.11** shows the provinces which possessed Estates (known as the *pays d'états*) and those which did not (the *pays d'élections*).

3.11

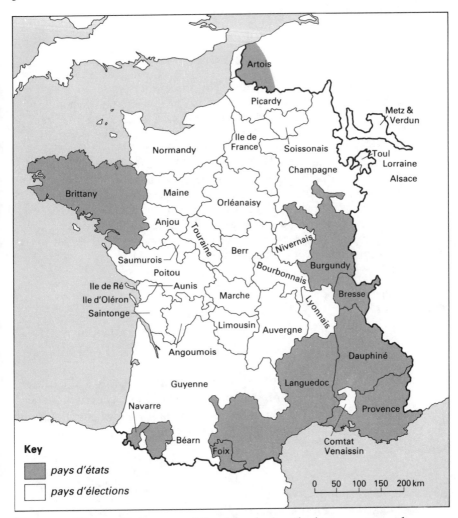

The *pays d'états* and the *pays d'élections* during the late seventeenth century

By far the most important difference between these regions was that in the *pays d'états* taxes could only be levied with the consent of the Estates, whereas in the *pays d'élections* the king did not need to consult with any provincial representatives. **3.12** is an extract from a memoir on the province of Languedoc, drawn up in 1698. It describes the composition of the Estates of Languedoc, and then analyses their rights, privileges and duties.

Although there were slight variations between the different *pays d'états*, all the characteristics described here were also true of other provincial Estates.

3.12

The Estates of Languedoc are composed of the three orders, that is to say: of the clergy, of the nobility, and of the third estate . . . The third estate is composed of the mayor-consuls appointed by the chief towns in each diocese[1] and by certain other places . . . The matters which are discussed by the Estates include the regulations for and the distribution of the taxes which are to be levied on the province; the examination of the closing statement by the treasurer of the general tax account, and those of the army and the equivalent; and other things of a similar nature which are reported to the Estates; and in general all topics which affect the province as a whole and public disorders in particular; and anything which might happen to damage their rights and privileges, of which by far the most important, and the one which the Estates regard as their fundamental principle, is that no tax can be imposed without their consent, just as no tax can be levied without the consent of the king.

[1] 'diocese': in Languedoc this term described an administrative rather than a religious division.

General Memoir on the Province of Languedoc, 1698, in Depping vol. I

In general, the King and the provincial Estates agreed easily and harmoniously on levels of taxation. For example, in **3.13**, two royal commissioners, the Prince de Conti and Bazin de Bezons, recount their negotiations with the Estates of Languedoc over the so-called 'free gift', a direct tax paid by all the *pays d'états*.

3.13

This morning Monseigneur le Prince de Conti came to the Estates . . . [and] told them that the King was pleased with the respectful way in which they had expressed their opinions in the first debate, when they offered 1,200,000 *livres*.[1] However, as this sum was not proportionate to the needs of the state, he had come to ask them to conclude by a second debate what they had begun by the first . . . Scarcely had Monseigneur le Prince de Conti left the assembly than the deputies came to him with the reply that they had unanimously agreed to give 1,400,000 *livres*. Monseigneur le Prince de Conti replied that the King had kindly granted him the power to accept this sum, in order to give some relief to the province, and in consideration of the efforts which they had made in previous years, but that this was on condition that the payments be made monthly. When this was reported to the assembly, the news was received with the greatest joy and warm appreciation of His Majesty's goodness . . .

¹ *'livres'* = French currency, valued at 100 *centimes* each.

The Prince de Conti and Bazin de Bezons to Colbert, 29 December 1663, in Depping vol. I

But the provincial assemblies were not always so co-operative. By far the most consistently difficult were the Estates of Brittany, which was a relatively late addition to the kingdom of France, and therefore anxious to preserve its own particular liberties. In 1674 the Breton Estates managed to secure the revocation of several royal edicts which had significantly eroded their right to determine levels of taxation and customs dues in Brittany, and had curtailed the powers of ancient noble courts which survived in large parts of the province. But – as a contemporary letter from Madame de Sévigné [3.14] shows – they had to pay a total of 5,200,000 *livres* in taxes and grants to the King for this concession. That was an unprecedented burden, representing nearly five times as much as the province had hitherto paid in any one year.

3.14

All the edicts which were strangling us in our province have been revoked. The day that Monsieur de Chaulnes¹ announced this, there was a cry of 'Long live the King' which reduced all members of the Estates to tears; they embraced each other and were beside themselves with joy; they ordered a *Te Deum*,² bonfires and a public expression of thanks to Monsieur de Chaulnes. But do you know how much we are giving to our King as a token of our gratitude? 2,600,000 *livres*³ and as much again for the free gift; that is exactly 5,200,000 *livres*. What do you think of that little sum? This gives you some idea of the kindness which has been shown to us in removing the edicts.

⁵

¹ *'Monsieur de Chaulnes'* = the Duc de Chaulnes, the Governor of Brittany.
² *'Te Deum'* = a Roman Catholic service of thanksgiving to God.
³ *'livres'*: see **3.13, note 1.**

Madame de Sévigné to Madame de Grignan, 1 January 1674, in Madame de Sévigné, *Lettres*, ed. Gérard-Gailly (3 vols., Paris, 1953–7) (hereafter cited as Madame de Sévigné, *Lettres*), vol. I

Questions

1 Comment on the location of the *pays d'états* shown in **3.11.**

2   Compare the location of the *pays d'états* [3.11] with that of the *parlements* [3.7]. Does any common pattern emerge? Discuss the value of this sort of evidence to the historian.

3   Use 3.12 to summarise the composition, rights and duties of the Estates of Languedoc.

4   Which of the following descriptions of 3.13–3.14 do you prefer, and why:
   (i)   'instances of co-operation between monarch and Estates, with both sides prepared to compromise'
   (ii) 'illustrations of Louis's ability to get his own way while granting minimal concessions'?

5   From the evidence in 3.11–3.14, to what extent were the Estates in the *pays d'états*:
   (i)   representative of the French people
   (ii) a limitation on the French monarch's authority?

6   Using 3.7–3.14, in which parts of France would you expect Louis to have most difficulty in imposing his authority? What evidence have you found, in this chapter and elsewhere, that this was the case?

However, when the King added three further taxes to the already heavy load, large parts of Brittany went into open revolt. This was the most serious insurrection during Louis's entire reign, and affords a case study in his handling of popular disorder. The Breton rebels identified three taxes – devised by Colbert in 1673 to finance the Dutch war – as their main grievances: a tax on stamped paper, and new impositions on tobacco and pewter. The first reports which reached the Governor of Brittany, the Duc de Chaulnes, described those responsible for the violence [3.15]. He wrote to Colbert on 22 April:

3.15

I am sending you the letters which I have just received by an express courier . . . sent from Rennes[1] . . . They show that at Rennes last Friday there was an uprising by a rabble of vagabonds, most of whom were outsiders; that the town did its duty and played no part, and that the few nobles who were there have expressed their devotion to the King's service . . .

[1] 'Rennes' = the principal town in Brittany, and the seat of the Breton Estates and *parlement*.

The Duc de Chaulnes to Colbert, 22 April 1675, in Depping vol. III

However, the Duc de Chaulnes's own investigations, reported to Colbert on 12 June, revealed a more sinister picture [3.16].

3.16

The true source of this uprising is the *parlement* . . . The procurators and other judicial officials have spread a thousand rumours against the King's authority, and such attitudes cannot be allowed to grow among people who are in a position of power . . . The remedy is to destroy completely the suburbs of this town. It is somewhat violent, but it is, in my opinion, the only way. It would not be difficult to   5 carry out with trained troops.

The Duc de Chaulnes to Colbert, 12 June 1675, in Depping vol. III

Moreover, there is evidence that other social groups were not entirely innocent. In 3.17, Madame de Sévigné describes the horrific punishment imposed on one rebel leader, and also his dying confession.

3.17

Would you like to hear the latest news from Rennes? The day before yesterday, a man named Violon, who had started the battle and the pillaging at the stamped-paper tax offices, was broken on the wheel. He was quartered after his death, and his four quarters were displayed at the four quarters of the town . . . As he was dying he said that it was the tax-farmers of the stamped-paper tax who had given   5 him twenty-five *écus*[1] to start this rebellion . . .

[1] '*écus*' = French coins, valued at three *livres*, or sixty *sous* each.

Madame de Sévigné to Madame de Grignan, 30 October 1675, in Madame de Sévigné, *Lettres*, vol. I

The Breton uprising became known as the 'stamped paper revolt', or alternatively as the 'revolt of the red caps', after the hats worn by some of the rebel leaders. The disorders soon spread from the area around Rennes in eastern Brittany into the western half of the province. Here the rebels in fourteen coastal parishes drew up a remarkable manifesto called the 'Peasant Code' in which they stated their principal demands [3.18].

3.18

That it is forbidden, on pain of being hanged from a gibbet, to give shelter to the salt-tax collector and to his children, and to provide them with food or with any other goods; on the contrary, it is prescribed that they be tormented as if by a mad

dog . . . That there be levied, for no matter what tax, not more than one hundred
sous[1] per hogshead of wine from outside, and one *écu*[2] for that from vineyards   5
within the province, provided that innkeepers and landlords shall sell the former at
five *sous* and the latter at three *sous* per quart . . . That justice shall be administered
by able men chosen from among our honourable citizens, who shall be paid a
salary, as shall their clerks, so that they cannot claim any fee for sitting from the
parties concerned, on pain of punishment; – and that stamped paper shall be held   10
in execration by them and their successors, to which end all the acts and writs
which have been written upon it shall be copied on to other paper and shall then be
burned, so that even the memory of stamped paper shall be entirely blotted out . . .
That the present regulations shall be read and published with the announcements
at high mass and in the square of every town and in every parish, and affixed to the   15
crosses which shall be placed there.

(Signed) The Skull-breaker and the People

[1] '*sous*' = French currency, valued at five *centimes* each.
[2] '*écu*': see 3.17, note 1.

**The Peasant Code, 2 July 1675, in A. de La Borderie, *La révolte du papier
timbré advenue en Bretagne en 1675: histoire et documents* (Saint-Brieuc,
1884)**

Although the government wished to be as lenient as possible, it took two
important steps to quell this revolt and to prevent another. First, the Breton
parlement was moved from Rennes to the much smaller town of Vannes.
Madame de Sévigné described this as 'a most grievous blow'. Second, an
army of about five thousand troops was sent to spend the autumn and
winter in Brittany. As a further letter [3.19] from the Duc de Chaulnes to
the Marquis de Louvois (the Superintendent of Postal Services) indicates,
this became a major punishment in itself to the province.

3.19

I cannot find words, Monsieur, to describe the destruction caused by the troops on
the march. The Queen's Battalion, leaving Rennes to go to Saint-Brieuc, has
pillaged every house within four leagues of its path between the two towns, and as
the troops' displeasure at not being allowed to do precisely as they want may lead
them to take some kind of revenge, I hope you will agree when I ask you to send   5
circular letters to each colonel and captain, ordering them to confine their cavalry
to their duties . . . Otherwise this province will be treated as if it were enemy
territory . . .

**The Duc de Chaulnes to the Marquis de Louvois, 9 February 1676, in
*La révolte dite du papier timbré ou des bonnets rouges en Bretagne en
1675*, ed. Jean Lemoine (Paris/Rennes, 1898)**

Questions

1 Account for the discrepancies between the different reports of who was responsible for the Breton revolt [3.15–3.17]. How much weight would you place on each, and why?

2 To what extent do 3.15–3.18 indicate that Breton society was united against the Crown? Explain your answer.

3 From the evidence in 3.15–3.18, what were the principal grievances which caused the Breton revolt? What other motives may there have been?

4 Comment on the 'remedy' advocated by the Duc de Chaulnes in 3.16.

5 How far does 3.18 demonstrate that this rebellion was a 'popular uprising'? Give reasons for your answer.

6 What does 3.19 tell you about:
   (i)   the personality and attitudes of the Duc de Chaulnes
   (ii) French military organisation in the late seventeenth century?

7 'A disastrous failure for which Brittany paid dearly.' Discuss this view of the 1675 revolt in the light of 3.15–3.19.

8 Using your broader knowledge of the period, how exceptional was the 1675 revolt, and the government's response to it?

9 Looking back to the previous chapter, can you explain why 1675 saw rebellion in Brittany but not in Dauphiné [2.14]?

But such harsh 'remedies' were expensive and unpleasant to apply. Louis's preferred strategy was to ensure that his laws and police force prevented disorders before they could turn into a full-scale insurrection. This was particularly evident in the administration of Paris. The size and importance of the capital ensured that the government was rather more closely involved in its affairs than in those of many lesser towns and cities. Moreover, the congestion and poverty of Paris presented considerable opportunities for violence and disaffection. The next four extracts [3.20–3.23] present some typical examples of measures designed to regulate the city's laws and to preserve public order. 3.20 is taken from a royal edict of March 1667 which established a lieutenant of police for Paris.

3.20

The lieutenant of police shall be responsible for the security of the city . . ., the carrying of weapons which have been forbidden by ordinance, the cleaning of streets and public places, together with adjacent buildings, the giving of the

necessary orders in time of fire or flood; equally for supervision of all the goods
needed for the sustenance of the city . . .; for inspecting the covered and open   5
markets and fairs, hostelries, inns, lodging houses, gambling dens, smoking
saloons and places of ill fame; for dealing with illicit gatherings, riots, revolts and
disorders . . .; for standardising the weights and scales of all communities in the
city and its suburbs, to the exclusion of all other judges; for hearing cases arising
from contravention of the ordinances, statutes and regulations about printing and   10
printers . . .

**Edict creating a Lieutenant of Police for Paris, March 1667, in Isambert
vol. XVIII**

The same meticulous attention to detail was apparent in an edict of
December 1672, which regulated the administration and commerce of
Paris [3.21].

3.21

Because of the singular affection which we feel for our loyal subjects, citizens and
inhabitants of Paris . . . we have ordered the rewriting of the ordinances, customs,
statutes and regulations of the mayor and aldermen of the said city, concerning its
government and administration, and the control of the sale of all goods which
arrive by river, and which are distributed on the quays, in the squares and in the   5
markets; which seemed to us to be even more necessary and useful in the said city
because the ancient ordinances dating back as far as 1415 have not been revised or
reformed, and are in several ways out of date . . .
[Then followed a series of detailed regulations concerning the maintenance of the
river and its banks; the rules for navigation on it; the unloading and sale of   10
merchandise; the duties of port and city officials; and the sale of grain, wines,
cider, fish, hay, timber, coal and charcoal.]

**Edict Concerning the Government of Paris, December 1672, in Isambert
vol. XIX**

Yet, however well regulated the government of Paris, there was always the
threat of disorder whenever large groups of people gathered together.
Theatres became a particular problem, and were the subject of an
ordinance in January 1674 [3.22].

3.22

It is forbidden for anybody, of whatever birth, condition and profession, to gather
and assemble in front of or around the places where plays are being presented; to
carry firearms, to attempt to force entry, to draw a sword and to commit any

violence or to excite any tumult, be it inside or outside, on pain of their lives, and of
extraordinary proceedings being taken against them, as disturbers of the peace and 5
public safety.

Ordinance for the Policing of Theatres, 9 January 1674, in Clément vol. VI

A further cause of anxiety were the many vagabonds, criminals and beggars
who gravitated to Paris from all over France. A General Poorhouse of Paris
had been founded in 1656, but soon became acutely overcrowded. In
March 1680, therefore, it was ordered to provide relief only for the young,
aged and infirm of the capital [3.23]. The able-bodied of all ages, and those
from outside Paris, had to find their own livelihood, and faced imprison-
ment if caught begging.

3.23

We have thought it reasonable to regulate on the one hand the sort of people who
must be admitted and looked after charitably inside this Poorhouse, and at the
same time to create new penalties which will make a stronger impression on the
minds of vagabonds . . . To this end we order that there shall be freely received
into this Poorhouse of our good city of Paris the poor children and the aged of   5
either sex, those suffering from epilepsy, fits and other ills of this nature, provided
that they were born or have lived for several years in . . . Paris, or its suburbs . . .
and cannot subsist without the help of the said Poorhouse . . . We further order
that all able-bodied persons of either sex, aged sixteen years or above, who have
the necessary strength to gain their own livelihood, and who are found begging in   10
the city and suburbs . . . of Paris . . . shall be confined in separate buildings for
each sex for a fortnight or longer as the directors shall judge appropriate, where
they shall be given only what is absolutely necessary for their survival, and shall be
employed on the harshest work which their bodies will stand. If such people are
found begging a second time, they shall be confined in the same place for three   15
months; if a third time, for a year; and if a fourth time, we order that they shall be
confined for the rest of their lives, never leaving, on whatever pretext, even in case
of illness . . .

**Regulations for the Administration of the General Poorhouse of Paris,
23 March 1680, in Isambert vol. XIX**

Questions

1 'Unjustified interference in the administration of Paris.' Discuss this
   view of **3.20–3.21.**
2 Why might theatres have been potential trouble spots [**3.22**]?

3   What attitudes to the poor emerge in 3.23? Would you describe them as
    charitable, harsh, or neither?

4   'The idea [of the General Poorhouse] was not to isolate the poor in
    order to protect the rich, but, rather, to restore human dignity to those
    on the fringes of society' (François Bluche). Does 3.23 bear out this
    judgement?

5   'Preventive medicine, designed to cure the danger of public disorder.'
    How far do you think this was the motive behind 3.20–3.23?

6   Do the extracts in this chapter suggest that Louis XIV sought radical
    changes in French society? If so, what were they?

7   Has this chapter modified your view of how far this was an 'absolutist'
    régime? Explain your answer.

8   'Local diversity within an absolutist framework.' Discuss this view of
    Louis XIV's France using material from this chapter, and your wider
    knowledge.

9   Using the material in this book, and elsewhere, assess the long-term
    impact of Louis XIV's reign on the development of French society.

4 Religious policies

Of all the subjects examined in this book, the one which requires the greatest imaginative leap is religion. It is vital to appreciate that the nature and significance of religion in seventeenth-century France were quite different from today. Above all, it was practically impossible to separate religion and politics. Religion was seen not as a private belief but as a public duty which shaped a person's attitudes towards a whole range of political, social, economic and moral questions. Furthermore, the idea of religious toleration was largely unknown, and it was thus extremely difficult for people of different beliefs to co-exist peacefully. An old French slogan 'une foi, une loi, un roi' (one faith, one law, one king) was widely thought to offer the only recipe for true stability. Religious discord had caused a series of bloody civil wars in France between 1562 and 1598. Under Louis XIV it was still a potential threat to public order and political harmony which no monarch could afford to neglect. In this chapter we will therefore examine the religious problems which Louis faced, the ways in which he tried to overcome them, and the extent to which he was successful.

His difficulties were essentially twofold. First, the relationship between the French Crown, the Catholic Church and the papacy remained highly controversial. As a result, conflicts within the French Church, or between the king and the Church, were liable to raise delicate questions about the respective powers of monarch and Pope. Second, since the mid-sixteenth century, France had contained a sizeable minority of committed Protestants (Huguenots). In a Catholic kingdom ruled by a Catholic monarch, these represented a possible source of dissent and subversion. Let us take each of these problems in turn.

In seventeenth-century France, many Catholics felt a patriotic pride in the so-called 'Gallican Liberties' – certain rights, dating from the early Middle Ages, which allowed the French Church some independence from papal authority. Traditionally, these unwritten 'Liberties' ensured that papal Bulls (edicts) could not be published in France without royal permission; that Roman courts had no authority over French subjects; and that French law courts had jurisdiction over ecclesiastical affairs. In 1516,

King Francis I and Pope Leo X had reached an agreement over these Gallican Liberties in the Concordat of Bologna, and this settlement survived until the French Revolution of 1789. Yet there was a significant minority of French clergy who associated Gallicanism with royal absolutism and insisted that the Pope was the source of all authority within the Church. These 'Ultramontanes' included the Jesuits and the Mendicant Friars, and constituted another potential threat to the Crown. Louis XIV's reign saw two major controversies which bitterly divided French Catholic clergy and disrupted his relations with the papacy.

The first arose over what was known as the *droit de régale*. This was the twofold right of the king to receive and administer the revenues of all French dioceses after the death of a bishop until his successor had taken an oath of fidelity to the monarch (the *régale temporelle*); and also to nominate clergy to all benefices normally controlled by the bishop (the *régale spirituelle*). French kings had claimed this right since the early Middle Ages, and Pope Leo X finally conceded it for certain parts of France in the Concordat of Bologna. But in February 1673 Louis XIV issued a decree which dramatically extended the *régale* [4.1].

4.1

The right of *régale* which we have in all churches of this kingdom is one of the oldest royal prerogatives . . . Nevertheless, the archbishops, bishops and chapters of the churches in several provinces, and particularly of those in Languedoc, Guyenne, Provence and Dauphiné, claim themselves exempt from it . . .
We wish our right to be universally recognised. For these reasons, we therefore   5
declare that the right of *régale* belongs to us universally in all the archbishoprics and bishoprics of our kingdom, and the lands under our rule, with the sole exception of those exempted by special royal decree . . . We therefore wish that archbishops and bishops be bound, within two months from their oath of fidelity to us, to obtain our letters patent of appointment, and to have them registered in our   1(
chambre des comptes[1] in Paris; and that those who have taken the oath of fidelity, and not obtained our letters of appointment, be required to obtain them and to have them registered within two months in our said *chambre des comptes*. If they fail to do this within the appointed time, the vacant benefices within their dioceses shall be subject to royal nomination under the *régale*.

[1] '*chambre des comptes*' = a 'sovereign court' for the handling of taxes.

Royal edict concerning the *régale*, 10 February 1673, in Isambert vol. XIX

Although Louis had no legal justification for this step, the vast majority of French archbishops and bishops complied with the new requirements. But

Bishop Pavillon of Alet and Bishop Caulet of Pamiers insisted that Louis was exceeding his rights and appealed to Pope Innocent XI. The Pope rushed to their defence, and protested in three strongly-worded brevets (papal letters) to Louis. 4.2 is an extract from the third brevet, issued on 29 December 1679.

4.2

We have already told Your Majesty clearly and repeatedly, in two earlier brevets, that your declaration of 1673 extending the *régale* to dioceses never before subject to it is harmful to the liberties of the Church, contrary to divine and human law, and in stark contrast to the practice of your predecessors . . . You must recognise in our letters the just grief and misery of all the bishops, and moreover you must   5
recognise the will of God, who speaks to you through us and warns you to revoke your edict and everything which has harmed the rights and liberty of the Church. If you do not do this, we are very much afraid that you will suffer divine vengeance, as we have said before, and which we now declare for the third time, although with regret, because of the tenderness which we feel for you. But we cannot resist the   10
will of God, which urges us to tell you this.

Pope Innocent XI to Louis XIV, 29 December 1679, in L.E. Dupin, *Histoire ecclésiastique du dix-septième siècle* (4 vols., Paris, 1714) (hereafter cited as Dupin), vol. III

Then the Pope made a serious miscalculation. When Bishop Caulet of Pamiers died in 1680, the Archbishop of Narbonne, who supported Louis's claims, tried to nominate the next bishop. This was well within the rights of a French archbishop. But in January 1681, Innocent XI declared the Archbishop's nomination illegal and threatened those who accepted it with excommunication. The majority of French clerics bitterly resented this invasion of the liberties of the Gallican Church, and petitioned Louis to call a General Assembly of the Clergy. The Assembly met in October 1681, and rapidly approved a royal edict in which Louis clarified the right of *régale* and described how he intended to use it [4.3]:

4.3

Nobody shall be presented by us and our successors to any vacant cathedral or collegiate church within our kingdom . . . unless they are of the age, qualifications and other qualities prescribed by the holy canons and by our ordinances . . . We wish those whom we present to these benefices to appear before the . . . bishops to obtain their approval and consecration before they undertake any duties . . . In   5
cases of refusal . . . we wish the said prelates to explain the reasons in writing to us,

C

so that we may provide other candidates . . . In this way, we intend to enjoy our
right of *régale* in the same way as previous kings, and as we have done until now . . .

**Royal edict concerning the *régale*, January 1682, in *Documents relatifs aux
rapports du clergé avec la royauté de 1682 à 1705*, ed. Léon Mention (Paris,
1893) (hereafter cited as Mention)**

Having accepted this edict, the French clergy addressed the following
letter to Innocent XI [4.4]:

4.4

Holy Father, our predecessors, those men so admirable for their sanctity and their
wisdom, have taught us that the security of states is based on the pious union
between monarchy and priesthood; and that when one of these powers attacks the
other, both are endangered; that when they quarrel justice and the peace of the
Church are ended within a state; that this causes schisms, scandals, the damnation   5
of souls; and that without this union nothing can remain secure among human
beings . . . This is why, Holy Father, humbly kneeling at your feet and awaiting
your apostolic blessing, we beg the Sovereign Author of the Church to inspire you
with counsels of peace, and to act entirely in the best interests of the Church, and
of your glory, so that your Holiness may follow your predecessors in working for   10
peace.

**The General Assembly of French Clergy to Pope Innocent XI, 3 February
1682, in Mention**

Questions

1   Explain and comment on the phrase 'one of the oldest royal preroga-
    tives' [4.1, lines 1–2].
2   How convincing do you find Louis's arguments in 4.1?
3   Does 4.2 constitute a reasonable response to 4.1? Explain your answer.
4   Comment on the tone of 4.2.
5   Why do you think 4.3 proved acceptable to the General Assembly of
    the French clergy in 1682?
6   Why might the French clergy have felt obliged to write 4.4?

The General Assembly then went a stage further. Colbert suggested that
this might be a good opportunity to settle once and for all the knotty
problem of relations between the Crown and the Pope. The Assembly was
initially reluctant, but after some government pressure endorsed four
propositions drawn up by Bishop Bossuet (see Chapter 1). These became

known as the Gallican Articles [4.5], and represented a skilful compromise between royal and papal powers.

4·5

1 ... Kings and princes are not subjected by the ordinance of God to any ecclesiastical authority in temporal affairs; nor by the authority of the keys of the Church can they be deposed, directly or indirectly, nor can their subjects be dispensed from loyalty and obedience or absolved from the oath of fidelity which they have taken ...   5
2 Full authority in spiritual matters is, however, inherent in the Apostolic See [= the papacy] and the successors of Peter, the Vicar of Christ [= the Popes] ...
3 Hence the exercise of the Apostolic authority should be moderated by the canons established by the Holy Spirit and consecrated by the respect of the   10 whole world ...
4 In questions of faith, the leading role is to be that of the Pope; and his decrees apply to all churches in general and to each of them in particular. But his judgement is not unchangeable, unless it receives the consent of the Church.

The Four Gallican Articles, 19 March 1682, in Mention

Three days later, Louis issued an edict requiring the Four Gallican Articles to be taught in churches and schools throughout France. Innocent XI, furious at what he regarded as the French clergy's betrayal of papal authority, refused to institute to benefices any priests who had attended the General Assembly. This directly contravened the Concordat of Bologna. Louis XIV retaliated by refusing to present any clergy who had not taken part in the Assembly. The result was total deadlock. By 1688 thirty-five French sees were without a bishop. That same year, Innocent XI excommunicated Louis's ambassador in Rome for abusing his diplomatic immunity, and finally excommunicated Louis himself. The King then seized the papal city of Avignon in October 1688, and there was even talk that the French Church might secede from Rome altogether. This was averted by the death of Innocent XI in August 1689 and the election of the much more conciliatory Alexander VIII (1689–91) and Innocent XII (1691–1700). A settlement was finally reached in 1693 when Innocent XII recognised those bishops who had attended the 1682 General Assembly (after they officially apologised), and Louis in return withdrew his edict requiring the Four Gallican Articles to be taught officially [4.6]. Thereafter, the issue of the *régale* was quietly dropped; and Louis in practice exercised all the powers which he claimed.

4.6

Very Holy Father, I always had high hopes that your advancement to the
pontificate would shower advantages upon the Church and our religion. I now see
with great joy all the great and good things which Your Holiness is doing for both.
This deepens my filial respect for Your Holiness, and as I search to give the
clearest proof of this, I wish to tell Your Holiness that I have ordered that my edict   5
of 22 March 1682 concerning the declaration made by the French clergy [= the
Four Gallican Articles] should no longer be observed. I desire not only to tell Your
Holiness of my feelings, but also that the whole world may see from this the
reverence which I feel for your venerable and holy qualities. I have no doubt that
Your Holiness will respond with clear signs of your fatherly affection for me, and I   10
pray that God may grant you health, happiness and long life.

Louis XIV to Pope Innocent XII, 14 September 1693, in Mention

Questions

1   Explain and comment on the phrase 'the authority of the keys of the
    Church' [4.5, lines 2–3].
2   Summarise the relative powers of the Pope and the King of France as
    laid down in 4.5. Which of them gained more from the Gallican
    Articles, and why?
3   Speculate on the motives which prompted Louis XIV to write 4.6.
4   From the evidence in this chapter, and your broader knowledge, why
    did the controversy over the *régale* last so long?
5   Who would have been more satisfied with the outcome of the *régale*
    controversy, the Gallicans or the Ultramontanes? Explain your answer.

The second major controversy within the Catholic Church under Louis
XIV surrounded the rise of Jansenism. This doctrine originated in
Augustinus, written by Cornelius Jansen, Bishop of Ypres (1585–1638) and
published posthumously in 1641. Strongly influenced by the writings of
Saint Augustine, Jansen argued that human beings were unable to achieve
salvation without God's grace, which was bestowed on very few. He thus
resembled Calvin and other Protestants in asserting that the free will of
men and women alone could not save them.

Jansenism proved deeply divisive among both clergy and laity. Many
found its austerity and emphasis on God's omnipotence attractive, and a
thriving Jansenist community grew up in the convent of Port-Royal des
Champs, near Versailles. Two of the greatest intellectuals of seventeenth-
century France, the mathematician and philosopher Blaise Pascal and the

poet and playwright Jean Racine, were both Jansenists. But there were others, particularly the Jesuits, who thought Jansenism denied the freedom and responsibility of individual Christians, and condemned it as the heresy of despair.

Throughout his reign, Louis remained firmly hostile to the Jansenists. Encouraged by his Jesuit confessors, he regarded them as troublemakers within the Church. Moreover, their emphasis on the role of ordinary priests and of the laity in Church affairs evoked a democratic spirit which upset his ideas of hierarchy and authority. This feeling was undoubtedly strengthened by the fact that many of the Crown's leading critics during the Frondes held Jansenist beliefs. Some steps against Jansenism had already been taken under Cardinal Mazarin. In May 1653, following a request by theologians at the Sorbonne, Pope Innocent X had condemned five Jansenist propositions in the Bull *Cum occasione*. Three years later, a General Assembly of the French clergy drew up a formulary against Jansenist tenets. But many French clergy – and especially the nuns of Port-Royal des Champs – refused to accept this formulary. Shortly after he assumed personal control of French government, Louis therefore decided on harsher measures to root out Jansenism. In his *Mémoires* for 1661, Louis wrote the following cryptic paragraph:

4.7

I applied myself diligently to the destruction of Jansenism and to the dissipation of the communities which fomented this novelty, [communities] which, though perhaps well intentioned, were ignorant of, or chose to ignore, the dangerous consequences which might ensue from it.

Mémoires de Louis XIV

To this end, in April 1661 the Council of State ordered all French clergy to sign the formulary against Jansenism, and all scholars and novices to leave Port-Royal des Champs. One of those novices, Marguerite Perrier, later recalled how these demands were perceived within the convent [4.8].

4.8

The enemies of Port-Royal had always said that the nuns concealed within their convent a Jansenist school . . . They had even invented the most fantastic and ridiculous stories about it. But these are completely untrue, and I can honestly say that when I left there in 1661 I was fifteen, and my sister seventeen, but we did not even know the names of the leading Jansenists, so that when we heard them

5

mentioned outside, we were entirely ignorant of who they were . . . The nuns were also ignorant, except for the superiors and some who had entered Port-Royal since these disputes began; but since they were not permitted to speak of what they had seen in the outside world, the others knew nothing of this. Proof positive of this is the fact that when the King's order of 1661 arrived, ordering the departure of all   10 scholars and novices . . . some of them believed that a great persecution had begun within the Church . . . and that they would have to renounce their religious vows entirely . . .

Reminiscences of Marguerite Perrier, in Charles Clémencet, *Histoire générale de Port-Roïal* (10 vols., Amsterdam, 1755–7), vol. IV

Those who signed the anti-Jansenist formulary thereby agreed to accept it 'purely and simply'. But the nuns of Port-Royal des Champs flatly refused, and were soon joined by the bishops of Angers, Beauvais, Alet and Pamiers. As we saw earlier, the last two also opposed Louis over the *régale*. In February 1665, at the King's request, Pope Alexander VII issued the Bull *Regiminis apostolici*, ordering all bishops, priests and nuns to sign the formulary. Louis then drafted an edict to enforce this, but had to hold a *lit de justice* (see Chapter 3) to secure its registration by the pro-Jansenist *parlement* of Paris. Still the four bishops and the nuns of Port-Royal des Champs refused to comply. Louis sought further papal assistance, and described the ensuing negotiations in his *Mémoires* [4.9].

4.9

I intended to complete the extirpation of the Jansenist sect, and after holding various councils for this purpose and procuring the best advice I could on such matters in the kingdom, I finally requested His Holiness to appoint commissioners to try the four bishops who had refused to comply with his Bull [*Regiminis apostolici*] and my declaration, in keeping with the traditional privileges of this   5 kingdom. And truly, I would never have expected that the Pope, who should be concerned about affairs of this nature, would have hesitated over this request; nevertheless I learnt that this proposal had met with grave difficulties . . . and I finally discovered that the court of Rome, imagining that I was extremely concerned by the threat of Jansenism, had concluded that it could sell me the   10 declarations that I desired at its own price . . . But to show the court of Rome that I had no other interest in this matter than that of the Church itself and that . . . I was not at all afraid of the Jansenists, I simply ordered the Duc de Chaulnes[1] to tell them . . . that I believed that I had done my duty, and that it was now up to the Pope to do his whenever he pleased.

[1] 'Duc de Chaulnes' = Louis's envoy to the Vatican in 1665–6, and later Governor of Brittany (see 3.15–3.19).

Mémoires de Louis XIV

Shortly afterwards, Alexander VII duly appointed commissioners to examine those who refused to sign the formulary. Ironically, the four bishops and the nuns of Port-Royal des Champs then adopted a Gallican stance by denying the Pope's right to interfere in this matter. Louis was thus enlisting papal authority against a group of his subjects who defended royal powers against Rome. The sides in this dispute had become extraordinarily confused. That they were eventually disentangled was due to Louis's third secretary, Hugues de Lionne, and to the election in 1667 of a more conciliatory Pope, Clement IX. Lionne suggested the recalcitrant bishops and nuns subscribe to the formulary 'sincerely' rather than 'purely and simply'. This form of words proved acceptable both to them and to Rome, and resulted in the so-called Peace of the Church of 1668. A letter from Clement IX to Louis XIV [4.10] completes this episode.

4.10

It is dear to our heart, and also our duty, to preserve with all possible care and diligence the peace and harmony of the whole Church. We have therefore learnt with great joy that the four bishops have agreed to submit 'sincerely' to the formulary. We are very pleased to see that you have accomplished this through clemency, rather than letting their disobedience provoke you to harshness. We   5
have seen, with unspeakable pleasure, the care and eagerness with which Your Majesty has given us this news . . . Therefore, with paternal affection and tenderness, we give you our apostolic blessing, and pray that God will crown your religious endeavours with glorious success, and grant you continual good fortune.

Pope Clement IX to Louis XIV, 29 September 1668, in Dupin vol. III

Questions

1   Explain and comment on the following phrases:
    (i) 'the extirpation of the Jansenist sect' [4.9, line 1]
    (ii) 'the traditional privileges of this kingdom' [4.9, lines 5–6].
2   What may be gleaned from 4.7 about Louis XIV's attitudes towards Jansenism?
3   Does 4.8 convince you that Louis's policy towards Port-Royal des Champs was mistaken? Explain your answer.
4   How far do 4.9–4.10 illustrate co-operation between Louis and the papacy over Jansenism? Consider the implications of your answer.
5   Why did Jansenism prove so divisive within the Catholic Church?
6   From the evidence here, and elsewhere, was the 1668 Peace of the Church likely to offer a permanent solution to the Jansenist controversy?

Unfortunately, the 'peace' established within the French Church in 1668 proved only temporary. It allowed the Jansenists to re-group their forces; and two Jansenist bishops (those of Alet and Pamiers) led the opposition to Louis's extension of the *régale*. Throughout the 1670s and 1680s, Louis was too preoccupied by his quarrel with Rome over the *régale* and by his campaign against the Huguenots (see below) to pay much attention to Jansenism. But once he had made his peace with Innocent XII in 1693 [4.6], the path was cleared for another offensive. Controversy flared up violently in 1701 when a Jansenist priest asked the theologians of the Sorbonne whether it was sufficient to hear condemnations of Jansen's *Augustinus* in 'respectful silence' – a purely formal deference which concealed private disapproval. All the old quarrels resurfaced, and in 1703 Louis wrote to Pope Clement XI, suggesting concerted action against Jansenism. The result was the papal Bull *Vineam Domini* (15 July 1705), which condemned 'respectful silence' outright. 4.11 is taken from Louis's edict ordering publication and observance of this Bull.

4.11

Because the greatest glory of a Most Christian king lies in using all the power which he has received from God to ensure constant observance of all the decisions of the Church, and because God has appointed us the defender and protector of the Church . . . we hereby declare . . . that the Bull [*Vineam Domini*] of our holy father the Pope be received and published throughout our kingdom, so that it may   5 be enforced and observed to the letter . . . In this way, peace will be lovingly and perfectly preserved, and the conflicts which have shattered it until now shall never be repeated . . .

Royal edict confirming the Bull *Vineam Domini*, 31 August 1705, in Dupin vol. IV

But this was not enough for Louis. Influenced by his second wife Madame de Maintenon (see below), and by his Jesuit confessors, the King apparently became more devout during his later years, more concerned to prove himself a loyal son of the Catholic Church. Furthermore, he attributed his military defeats in the War of the Spanish Succession (see Chapter 5) to God's anger, and wished to do everything possible to allay this. The nuns at Port-Royal des Champs – who refused to accept the terms of *Vineam Domini* – were an obvious target. Louis decided to end forever this standing insult to royal and papal authority, and in October 1709 ordered a dawn raid on the convent. The Marquise d'Huxelles

(1626–1712), mother of one of Louis's most senior generals, told the governor of the town of Furnes, the Marquis de la Garde, what happened next [4.12].

4.12

Eight days ago . . . Monsieur d'Argenson [the lieutenant of police for Paris] presented himself at the gates of Port-Royal des Champs in the King's name. They were thrown open to him, and when the King's wishes were made known to the Mother Prioress she assembled the chapter so as to tell them the news. This lasted until midday without any disturbance or tears from the nuns, but a respectful silence and submission to his orders. The Prioress asked Monsieur d'Argenson if he would allow them enough time to collect their meagre belongings. He replied that he had received no instructions about this from the King, but would take the responsibility himself. She thanked him and said that as there was no order the only thing to do was to leave with nothing but a staff and a breviary.[1] There were eight carriages and some chairs, in which these poor people were put. Troops have been left in the convent to guard it . . . The nuns have scarcely eaten since, for the sisters were only allowed to bring a little bread and wine. Here, Sir, is something to reflect upon when you pray to God . . .

[1] 'breviary' = a book used in the Roman Catholic Church containing the daily office.

The Marquise d'Huxelles to the Marquis de la Garde, 5 November 1709, in *Journal du Marquis de Dangeau*, **ed. M. Soulié** *et al.* **(19 vols. in 9, Paris, 1854–9), vol. XIII**

The attack on Port-Royal des Champs did not end there. On 22 January 1710 Louis ordered the convent to be demolished. The secular buildings were torn down in 1710–11, and the church in 1712. Even the nuns' cemetery was dismantled and the bodies exhumed. Yet Jansenist ideas proved much harder to destroy. Their appeal had been strengthened by a book entitled *Moral Reflections on the New Testament*, published in 1671 by a Jansenist priest, Pasquier Quesnel (1634–1719). Again Louis sought papal aid; and on 8 September 1713 Clement XI issued the Bull *Unigenitus* condemning Quesnel's book together with a long list of alleged Jansenist beliefs [4.13]. Ironically, the main resistance to this Bull came from the Gallicans, who attacked it as papal interference. Nevertheless, Louis accepted and enforced *Unigenitus*, and this effectively marked the end of Jansenism as a major influence within the French Church. By the end of his reign, Louis was thus working with an outside power, the papacy, to heal divisions at home.

4.13

We cannot applaud enough the zeal of our most dear son in Jesus Christ, Louis, the Most Christian King of France . . . For the defence and preservation of the purity of the Catholic faith, and for the extirpation of heresy . . . he has strongly solicited us to provide a speedy remedy, by our apostolic authority . . . Therefore, by virtue of this authority, we do once again forbid and condemn the said book   5
[= Quesnel's *Moral Reflections*], with what title or in what language soever it is printed, in whatever edition or version it has been published, or may be published hereafter (which God forbid). We condemn it as very apt to seduce simple souls, by words full of sweetness and by blessings . . . that is to say, by appearing to be a work full of piety. We likewise condemn all other books, whether in manuscript or   10
print, or (which God forbid) that may hereafter be printed in defence of the said book. We forbid all the faithful to read, copy, keep, retain or make any use of them, under pain of excommunication, which shall be incurred, *ipso facto*, by the disobedient. We also command our venerable brethren the archbishops and bishops, and the inquisitors of heresy, to suppress by censures, by the aforesaid   15
penalties, and by all other remedies of right and property, those who refuse to obey; and to this end, also to seek if necessary the assistance of the secular power . . .
[Then followed a denunciation of 101 specific beliefs attributed to the Jansenists]

Pope Clement XI, the Bull *Unigenitus*, 8 September 1713, in *Constitution de nostre saint père le Pape Clément XI du 8 de Septembre 1713, en Latin et Français* (Paris, 1713)

Questions

1   What does 4.11 reveal about Louis XIV's attitudes towards the Church and the papacy?

2   Do you think 4.12 is an unbiased account of the raid on Port-Royal des Champs? Explain your answer and consider its implications.

3   How far do Louis's words in 4.11 and his acceptance of 4.13 mark a betrayal of Gallicanism?

4   Consider the arguments for and against Louis's campaign against Jansenism.

5   What was the relationship between Jansenism and the opposition to Louis's extension of the *régale*?

6   Compare and contrast the attitudes of Gallicans and Ultramontanes towards the French Crown during the course of Louis XIV's reign.

7   Did the Catholic Church in France become more or less united under Louis XIV?

Finally, we turn to the problem of France's Protestant minority, the Huguenots. In the wake of the Reformation, Protestant ideas had gained a considerable following in France, to the anger of Catholics. Neither side was prepared to compromise, and as a result France had been torn by a series of internal wars of religion during the late sixteenth century. These conflicts eventually ended after the Protestant King Henry IV (1589–1610) was received into the Catholic Church in 1595. He thus became an acceptable ruler to both Catholics and Protestants, although France still remained bitterly divided between the two faiths. In a bid to secure political and religious harmony, Henry therefore issued the Edict of Nantes (13 April 1598) which permitted members of the 'so-called reformed religion' ('la religion prétendue réformée') to worship freely in certain parts of France, allowed them to hold public office, and granted them equality before the law with Catholics. Although the Huguenots lost their political privileges following an abortive coup in 1629, they retained their own schools, clergy and churches. By the early 1660s France contained around one million Huguenots – with six or seven hundred churches – in a total population of about twenty million.

An extract from Louis's *Mémoires* [4.14] suggests that he initially accepted this situation, provided that the Huguenots remained peaceful. However, he probably hoped that such a gentle approach would encourage some Huguenots to convert to Catholicism.

4.14

I believed . . . that the best way to reduce gradually the number of Huguenots in my kingdom was not to oppress them at all by any new rigour against them, but to implement what they had obtained during previous reigns, yet also to grant them nothing further and even to restrict its execution to the narrowest limits which justice and humanity would permit. I named for this purpose, from that very year   5
[= 1661] commissioners to execute the Edict of Nantes. I carefully put a stop everywhere to the enterprises of those of that religion, as in the Faubourg Saint-Germain [= a suburb of Paris], where I learnt that they were beginning to set up secret assemblies and schools for their sect; at Jamets in Lorraine, where, having no right of assembly, they had taken refuge in large numbers during the   10
disorders of the war and were holding their services there; at La Rochelle,[1] where the old inhabitants who were permitted to live there had little by little attracted a number of others, whom I obliged to leave.

[1] 'La Rochelle' = the large Huguenot community on the west coast of France.

Mémoires de Louis XIV

During the early years of Louis's reign, French Protestants were able to worship freely within designated areas; and relations with their Catholic neighbours were mostly amicable. 4.15 is taken from John Locke's description of the Protestants at Montpellier in February 1676.

4.15

The Protestants have here common justice generally, unless it be against a new convert [to Catholicism], whom they [= the courts] will favour. They pay no more taxes than their neighbours, are only incapable of public charges and offices. They have had within these ten years at least 160 churches pulled down. They and the papist laity live together friendly enough in these parts. They sometimes get and   5 sometimes lose proselytes [= converts]. There is nothing done against those that come over to the reformed religion, unless they be such as have before turned papists and relapse: these sometimes they prosecute. The number of Protestants in these latter years neither increases nor decreases much. Those that go over to the Church of Rome are usually drawn away by fair promises that most commonly fail   10 them, or else money if they be poor. The Protestants live not better than the Papists.

Locke's Travels

However, as Louis's reign progressed, his policy towards the Huguenots gradually hardened. The early 1680s saw a concerted effort to suppress Protestant worship in private and to ban Protestants from certain professions. In December 1686, all Protestant services were forbidden where the local Huguenot community consisted of fewer than ten families. Finally, in October 1685, Louis revoked the Edict of Nantes completely.

Historians have disagreed sharply about why Louis abandoned his earlier policy of toleration towards Protestants. There are five main theories:

1 the removal of religious diversity would promote social and political harmony within France at a time when Louis was increasingly preoccupied with foreign wars;
2 following his dispute with the papacy over the *régale*, Louis was anxious to re-establish his credentials as a loyal son of Rome;
3 Louis's ideal all along was 'one faith, one law, one king' (see above). He therefore desired the removal of French Protestants, and when gentle inducements failed to achieve this he resorted to harsher methods;
4 those gentle inducements included significant financial benefits for Huguenots who converted to Catholicism, such as pensions and tax

exemptions. This was an unwelcome burden on the state, especially during wartime;

5 his second wife, Madame de Maintenon, whom Louis had married secretly in 1683, was a devout Catholic who regarded Protestants as heretics and encouraged the King to curtail their rights.

It is likely that each of these motives inclined Louis to abolish the rights of French Protestants. But how did he justify this dramatic step in public? **4.16a** is taken from the preamble to the Edict of Fontainebleau which revoked the Edict of Nantes. This is followed by some extracts from the principal clauses [**4.16b**].

4.16a

King Henry [IV] . . . desiring to prevent the peace which he had procured for his subjects . . . from being disturbed because of the so-called reformed religion . . . arranged the policy which was to be adopted towards those of the said religion, the places in which they could practise it, and established special judges to administer justice for them . . . We now see with proper gratitude, which we owe to God, that   5 our efforts have achieved the end which we had sought, for the better and more numerous part of our subjects of the . . . so-called reformed religion has embraced the Catholic religion; and because, as a result of this, the execution of the Edict of Nantes, and of everything which has been enacted in favour of the said so-called reformed religion, becomes useless, we have judged that we could do nothing   10 better to wipe out entirely the memory of the disorders, of the confusion, of the evils which the progress of this false religion has caused in our kingdom . . . than to revoke completely the said Edict of Nantes.

4.16b

1   . . . All temples [= churches and chapels] of the people of the . . . so-called reformed religion situated in our kingdom, lands and lordships obedient to us should be demolished forthwith.

2   We forbid our subjects of the so-called reformed religion to assemble any more for public worship of the above-mentioned religion, in any place or   5 private house, under whatever pretext . . .

3   We likewise forbid all lords, of whatever rank they may be, to carry out heretical services in houses and fiefs [= noble estates] . . .

4   We order all ministers of the said so-called reformed religion who do not wish to be converted and to embrace the Catholic, Apostolic and Roman religion, to   10 depart from our kingdom . . . within fifteen days from the publication of our present edict . . . on pain of the galleys . . .

7   We prohibit private schools for the instruction of the children of the so-called reformed religion . . .

The Edict of Fontainebleau, October 1685, in Isambert vol. XIX

Another revealing source are the official medals issued to commemorate
the revocation. 4.17 was one of the most striking. Its obverse side [4.17a]
shows Louis XIV's profile with an inscription proclaiming him 'The Most
Christian King'; while on the reverse side [4.17b] a female figure,
representing true religion, tramples on Protestant heresy, symbolised by a
corpse holding a burnt-out torch.

4.17

A   B

The inscriptions read:
(A)   LVDOVICVS MAGNVS REX CHRISTIANISSIMVS [Louis the Great,
      Most Christian King]
(B)   EXTINCTA HAERESIS. EDICTUM OCTOBRIS M.DC.LXXXV
      [Heresy extinguished. The edict of October 1685]

**Medal commemorating the Edict of Fontainebleau, viewed on both sides,
October 1685, in L'Académie Royale des Médailles et des Inscriptions,**
Médailles sur les principaux événements du règne de Louis le Grand, **avec
des explications historiques (Paris, 1702)**

Questions

1   Explain and comment on the following phrases:
    (i)   'the so-called reformed religion' [4.16a, line 2]
    (ii) 'Heresy extinguished' [4.17b].
2   From the evidence in 4.14, what was Louis XIV's attitude towards French Protestantism in the short and the long term?
3   What may be learnt from 4.15 about the status and condition of French Protestants during the 1670s?
4   What arguments does Louis advance in 4.16a for the revocation of the Edict of Nantes?
5   How far do 4.16a–b mark a shift from Louis's position in 4.14? Explain your answer.
6   What do 4.17a–b reveal about how Louis wished the revocation to be perceived? Does this confirm or conflict with other evidence which you have seen in this chapter, and elsewhere?
7   How can the revocation of the Edict of Nantes be related to the controversies over the *régale* and Jansenism?
8   From the material in this chapter, and your wider reading, what were the most important considerations which prompted Louis to revoke the Edict of Nantes?

No act of Louis XIV's career has inspired such fulsome praise or such bitter condemnation as the Edict of Fontainebleau. Madame de Sévigné thought it 'sublime', while the French Catholic clergy were unanimous in welcoming the attack on 'heretics'. For the Jesuit and Court preacher Louis Bourdaloue (1632–1704) it represented the King's crowning achievement. Preaching in the chapel at Versailles on 1 November 1686, Bourdaloue declared:

4.18

I address these words to a king who, in order to triumph over the enemies of his state, has accomplished miracles of such renown that posterity will not credit it . . . and who, in order to triumph over the enemies of the Church, is today performing such miracles of zeal that we who witness them can scarcely believe our eyes, so much do they exceed our hopes. I am speaking to a king raised up and chosen by   5
God for things of which his august ancestors did not even dare to think, because he alone could have planned them and carried them out. This zeal for the interests

of God and the true worship of God is, Sir, that which sanctifies kings and which should be the apogee of your glorious destiny.

Louis Bourdaloue, sermon preached on 1 November 1686, in *Sermons du Père Bourdaloue*, ed. François Bretonneau *et al.* (17 vols., Paris, 1723–78), vol. XII

The poet and official propagandist Jean Le Clerc was similarly effusive in his praise of the revocation. 4.19 is an extract from his poem entitled 'The Triumph of the Faith'.

4.19

If this hydra that your hand has strangled
Does not provide to your virtue the worthiest of trophies
Then think of the cruel misfortunes that this sect has caused,
See how it has divided your subjects,
Consider in your heart its fatal practices.   5
How much blood poured forth, how many tragic stories of
The sacrileges of profaned altars.
Priests scorned and degraded, temples destroyed,
Blasphemies carried up to the sanctuary,
By all this see what it had been able to do.   10
To purge the state of an internal pestilence
Louis saw that it was time to cut its roots.
He broke the edicts by which our recent kings
Allowed this serpent the right to speak
From which never ceased to come its false maxims   15
Infecting minds and fomenting crimes.

Jean Le Clerc, *Le Triomphe de la Foy* (Paris, 1686)

The reaction of French Protestants, on the other hand, was bitterly hostile. Their feelings were summed up by the writer and minister Jean Claude, one of many Huguenots who fled to England [4.20].

4.20

We protest against the . . . revocation of the Edict of Nantes as a manifest abuse of the king's justice, authority and royal power, since the Edict of Nantes was in itself inviolable and irrevocable, above the reach of any human power, designed for a standing agreement and concordat between the Roman Catholics and us, and a fundamental law of the realm, which no authority on earth has power to infringe or   5 annul . . . But above all we protest against that impious and abominable position,

which is nowadays made the general rule in France, by which religion is made to
depend on the pleasure and despotic power of a mortal prince, and perseverance
in the faith branded with the names of rebellion and treason, which is to make of a
man a God, and tends to the introducing and authorising of atheism and idolatry.   10
We protest moreover against all manner of violent and inhumane detaining of our
brethren in France, whether in prisons, gallies, monasteries or any other
confinements, to hinder them from leaving the kingdom, and going to [seek] in
foreign countries that liberty of conscience they cannot enjoy in their own; which is
the utmost pitch of brutish cruelty and hellish iniquity.

**Jean Claude, *A Short Account of the Complaints and Cruel Persecutions of
the Protestants in the Kingdom of France*, trans. H. Reneu (London, 1707)**

In all, nearly 1,500 Huguenots were sent to the galleys, while a further
200,000 sought refuge in England, Switzerland and Holland. Many
foreign Protestants were appalled at their plight, particularly when they
witnessed the effects of Louis's policy at first hand. Gilbert Burnet
(1643–1715), who was Bishop of Salisbury from 1689 until his death,
travelled extensively in France during the mid-1680s, and left this
eye-witness account of Huguenot sufferings after the revocation of the
Edict of Nantes:

4.21

I went over the greatest part of France while it was in its hottest rage, from
Marseilles to Montpellier and from thence to Lyons, and so to Geneva. I saw and
knew so many instances of their injustice and violence that it exceeded even what
could have been well imagined; for all men set their thoughts on work to invent
new methods of cruelty. In all towns through which I passed, I heard the most   5
dismal accounts of those things possible, but chiefly at Valence, where one
Dherapine [= an *intendant*] seemed to exceed even the furies of Inquisitors. One
in the streets could have known the new converts, as they were passing by them, by
a cloudy dejection that appeared in their looks and deportment. Such as
endeavoured to make their escape, and were seized, (for guards and secret agents   10
were spread along the whole roads and frontier of France) were, if men,
condemned to the gallies, and, if women, to monasteries. To complete their
cruelty, orders were given that such of the new converts as did not at their death
receive the sacrament, should be denied burial, and that their bodies should be left
where other dead carcasses were cast out, to be devoured by wolves and dogs . . .   15
The greatest part of the clergy . . . were so transported with the zeal that their king
showed on this occasion, that their sermons were full of the most inflamed
eloquence that they could invent, magnifying their king in strains too indecent and
blasphemous to be mentioned by me.

Gilbert Burnet, *History of His Own Times* (2 vols., London, 1724–34), vol. I

Questions

1 Explain and comment on the following phrases:
   (i)   'miracles of zeal' [4.18, line 4]
   (ii) 'To purge the state of an internal pestilence' [4.19, line 11]
   (iii) 'a fundamental law of the realm' [4.20, lines 4–5].
2 Summarise the arguments for the revocation of the Edict of Nantes as laid out in documents 4.18–4.19.
3 Summarise the arguments against the revocation of the Edict of Nantes as laid out in documents 4.20–4.21.
4 Does 4.18 constitute evidence for Gilbert Burnet's claim in 4.21, lines 16–19?
5 Consider the view that documents 4.18–4.21 tell us as much about the people who wrote them as about the revocation of the Edict of Nantes.
6 From the evidence presented in this chapter, and elsewhere, to what extent was the ideal of 'one faith, one law, one king' a growing reality under Louis XIV? Explain your answer.
7 'Yet another aspect of his obsessive pursuit of absolute power.' Discuss this verdict on Louis's religious policies.
8 Did Louis's actions do more to promote religious harmony or religious discord within France?
9 In what ways did Louis's religious policies reinforce or obstruct his policies in other areas? Consider the implications of your answer.

5 Foreign policy

Louis XIV's foreign policy is a vast subject and a long book could easily be written on it alone. During the course of his reign France permanently replaced Spain as the dominant power in Europe. Yet the cost of this was enormous. Louis was at war for a total of thirty years between 1661 and 1715: against Spain in 1667–8 (the War of Devolution); against the United Provinces, Spain and the Empire in 1672–8 (the Dutch War); against the United Provinces, Great Britain, the Empire, Spain and several German states in 1689–97 (the Nine Years' War); and finally against the United Provinces, Great Britain, the Empire, Savoy, Brandenburg and Portugal in 1701–13 (the War of the Spanish Succession).

The diplomatic and military history of these conflicts is extraordinarily tangled. Furthermore, the international treaties which terminated them reveal a complex story of French gains and losses which makes it difficult to see any of them as either an outright victory or an outright defeat. In this chapter it is possible only to present a series of case studies, spotlighting particular themes and episodes. The sections which follow will examine in turn Louis's general approach to foreign policy as perceived by himself and others; his policy of *réunions* which precipitated the Nine Years' War; and the two Partition Treaties which formed the prelude to the War of the Spanish Succession.

Louis's own attitudes should be seen in the context of two contemporary assumptions. First, international relations in this period were perceived not as impersonal interactions between states, but as the outcome of personal or dynastic relationships between individual rulers. This meant that wars and treaties were often seen rather like private quarrels and agreements between sovereigns. Second, there was a prevalent belief that the defence of national security in diplomacy and war should be a monarch's top priority. Foreign policy was the statesman's natural sphere of activity. It is against this background that we can assess Louis's beliefs as recorded in his *Mémoires*. Document **5.1**, in which Louis sums up his general attitudes towards foreign policy, was written in 1662.

5.1

Do not doubt that at all times, and especially . . . in my younger days, I would have preferred to conquer states rather than acquire them. But . . . variety is necessary in glory as in everything else, and in that of princes more than in that of private individuals, for whoever says 'great king' means almost all the talents of his best subjects. Valour is one of these principal qualities, but it is not the only one, [for] it   5 leaves much to justice, to prudence and to good conduct, and to ability in negotiations . . . Always be in a position, my son, to inspire fear by arms, but only employ them if necessary, and remember that our power, even when it is at its height, must be infrequently tested in order to be at its most feared.

Mémoires de Louis XIV

Four years later, Louis developed these points further, and explored the connection between foreign policy and 'the glory of a prince' [5.2]. In particular, he reflected on the desirability of war against both Great Britain and Spain, and went on to explain why he eventually decided not to tackle both these powers simultaneously:

5.2

On the one hand, I imagined with pleasure the prospect of these two wars as a vast field which would provide great opportunities for me to distinguish myself. So many brave people whom I saw enthusiastic for my service seemed to be constantly urging me to provide some scope for their valour . . . But on the other hand, I knew that, just as a prince acquires glory by overcoming difficulties which he   5 cannot avoid, so he risks being accused of recklessness if he throws himself too readily into crises which a little skill might have spared him; that the greatness of our courage must not make us neglect our reason, and that the more dearly one loves glory, the more one must try to achieve it safely; . . . that to attack these two powerful enemies simultaneously would be to create a bond between them which   10 could not be dissolved at will . . . I was for some time uncertain between these two opinions. But if the first appealed more to my heart, the second satisfied my reason better; and I believed that in my post I had to sacrifice my inclinations in order to pursue the interests of my crown.

Mémoires de Louis XIV

Louis clearly ascribed a great deal of importance to this kind of strategic decision, and was anxious to pass on his own experience to the Dauphin. Yet he also believed that some features of international relations were so firmly established as to be unchangeable. These immovable landmarks included the hostility between France and Spain, which Louis described as follows in 1661:

5.3

The state of the two crowns of France and Spain today is such . . . that one cannot be exalted without the other being humbled. This creates a feeling of jealousy between them which is, dare I say, essential, and a sort of permanent enmity which treaties can mask but never extinguish, because its foundation is always there . . . As much, my son, as you must recognise that a superior power [= God] is capable   5 of upsetting your best laid plans when it so wishes, always rest assured . . . that having itself established the natural order of things, it will not often upset it, either in your favour or to your prejudice.

Mémoires de Louis XIV

Questions

1   Why might Louis 'have preferred to conquer states rather than acquire them' [5.1, lines 1–2]?
2   Use 5.1–5.2 to summarise how Louis thought foreign policy could assist a monarch's pursuit of 'glory'.
3   Are Louis's aims in 5.1–5.3 consistent or inconsistent? Explain your answer.
4   'The rationalisation of self-interest.' Is this a fair description of 5.1–5.3?
5   From the material elsewhere in this book, and your wider reading, are Louis's attitudes in 5.1–5.3 surprising or unsurprising, given his views on other matters? Justify your answer.
6   Was Louis's general approach to foreign policy typical or untypical of the age in which he lived? Explain your response.

However, Louis's enemies saw things very differently. Many concluded that he had no consistent principles beyond his own aggrandisement, and as a result could never be trusted. For example, in 1684 the German mathematician, scientist and philosopher Gottfried Wilhelm Leibniz (1646–1716), who travelled extensively around Europe, wrote a bitter satire of Louis's foreign policy called 'Mars Christianissimus' [5.4]. This title, which means 'Most Christian God of War', was a parody of the name traditionally adopted by French monarchs, 'Most Christian King'.

5.4

Since [the Peace of the Pyrenees]¹ has been broken and trampled underfoot at the first opportunity, it must be recognised that whoever henceforth trusts the word of

France is very stupid, and deserves to be deceived. That is why the Dutch, the Spanish, the Emperor and the other allies who negotiated at Nijmwegen[2] will sooner or later be punished for their credulity . . . We have seen that [Louis's]   5
aims went further than mere bravado . . . and that the ambition of the King was quite egocentric and looked as much to profit as to glory.

[1] 'the Peace of the Pyrenees' = the treaty between France and Spain signed in October 1659.
[2] 'negotiated at Nijmwegen': the Peace of Nijmwegen, concluded in August/September 1678, ended the Dutch War.

Gottfried Wilhelm Leibniz, 'Mars Christianissimus', in *Oeuvres de Leibniz*, ed. A. Foucher de Careil (7 vols., Paris, 1859–75), vol. III

Twenty-five years later, during the War of the Spanish Succession, an anonymous 'Life and History' of Louis XIV was published in London [5.5]. This hinted that Louis was a coward and then discussed the consequences of his overweening ambition.

5.5

We shall not find [Louis XIV] to be so great a man as the world has believed him to be. I have already insinuated that his personal valour is much suspected; but he has left no room to doubt of the height of his ambition, of which his whole history is one continued proof. But instead of the real valour and grandeur of soul, so natural to ambitious men, the efforts he has used to be thought the man he really is not   5
ha[ve] exposed his weakness and his vanity to all Europe. Which contagion from the throne has so affected the people [who] . . . increase and magnify (as they fancy) the glory of their prince, which they hardly seem to think inferior to that of God Almighty. Nor have they ever spared to do this even at the expense of their best allies . . . It [is] known to all Christendom that he has ever been its common   10
disturber.

[Anonymous], *The Life and History of Lewis XIV, present King of France and Navarre* (London, 1709)

Questions

1 Explain and comment on the following phrases:
   (i) 'the King . . . looked as much to profit as to glory' [**5.4, lines 6–7**]
   (ii) 'his personal valour is much suspected' [**5.5, line 2**].
2 Are **5.4–5.5** presenting similar or different criticisms of Louis XIV's foreign policy? Explain your answer.

3 The authors of 5.4–5.5 both came from countries which fought several wars against Louis. How does this affect the use of these sources by historians?

4 To what extent did Louis's proclaimed ideals [5.1–5.3] naturally give rise to the sort of charges made in 5.4–5.5?

5 From the materials in this book so far, and your wider reading, how fair are the accusations in 5.4–5.5?

In order to assess how far Louis put his maxims into practice, and whether or not the jibes of his enemies were fair, let us now examine two cameos of his foreign policy in action. The first is the so-called policy of *réunions*, pursued during the early 1680s. The Peace of Nijmwegen, which ended the Dutch War, had ceded a large part of the Spanish Netherlands to France. Nevertheless, Louis still felt vulnerable on his north-eastern and eastern frontiers – bordering on the Spanish Netherlands and the Holy Roman Empire – and wished to strengthen them even further. It was apparently Louis's Minister of War, the Marquis de Louvois, who first suggested the idea of *réunions*. In a confidential letter to Jacques de la Grange, *intendant* of Alsace, dated 17 February 1679, Louvois wrote:

5.6

I need a very powerful memory to tell me the names of all the villages which the King did not possess in 1672, which are situated between the Bishopric of Bale, Franche-Comté, Lorraine, the Rhine, the Saar and the lands of the Elector Palatine . . . [and] what you know of those who claim sovereignty over them . . . I will say, strictly between us, that I intend to use this information to alert the King 5 to whatever he can rightfully possess under the peace terms [of Nijmwegen], which gives the King the right to claim complete sovereignty over ten towns within Alsace, the villages which depend upon them, and all the fiefs [= lands] in Alsace which until now have been claimed as lands of the Empire . . .

The Marquis de Louvois to Jacques de la Grange, *intendant* of Alsace, 17 February 1679, in Georges Livet, *L'intendance d'Alsace sous Louis XIV, 1648–1715* (Strasbourg, 1956)

Louis keenly accepted Louvois's advice, and declared that certain lands once French but later lost were dependencies of areas which he ruled under the Treaties of Nijmwegen, and therefore rightfully his. To this end, 'chambers of reunion' were set up by the *parlements* at Breisach, Besançon and Metz which then confirmed the King's alleged rights to various territories on the left bank of the Rhine. Louis used these confirmations to justify several annexations (or *réunions*). A typical example was a decree annexing the County of Chiny [5.7] which Louis issued on 21 April 1681. The county was at that time a fief of the Duchy of Luxembourg; but careful research by the French Attorney General apparently proved otherwise.

5.7

Louis, by the grace of God King of France and Navarre, to the chief officer of the chamber which we have established in our town of Metz . . . our Attorney General has uncovered that it appears from several titles and documents that the County of Chiny, with its dependencies, is a territory which has always been under our protection and still is today, according to the law and custom of Beaumont-en-   5
Argone of which we are sovereign. And that the said County of Chiny with its dependencies is a fief of the Duchy of Bar, of which we are the sovereign, and that the people of the said County of Chiny have for a long time taken their lawsuits to Montmédy, a town which . . . was ceded to us by the Treaty of the Pyrenees in 1659, and confirmed by the Treaties of Nijmwegen in 1679. Our Attorney   10
General has therefore concluded from this investigation that the so-called lord of the County of Chiny should within a month take an oath of loyalty to us and pay homage to us in person.

Extrait des registres de la Chambre Royalle establie à Metz, 21 April 1681 (Metz, 1681)

The first *réunion* was that of Montbéliard, decreed by the *parlement* at Besançon in August 1680. Over the following four years, more and more regions, towns and cities were claimed as French 'dependencies' and promptly annexed. Map 5.8 shows the areas affected.

5.8

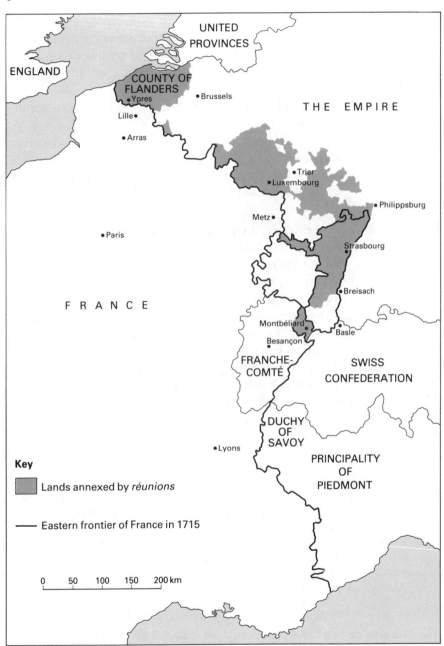

Lands annexed by Louis XIV's *réunions*, 1680–84

Questions

1 How far do 5.7–5.8 indicate that Louis took the policy of *réunions* further than Louvois had intended? Explain your answer.
2 'Armed aggression beneath a thin veneer of legal pretence.' From the evidence in 5.6–5.8, and your wider reading, is this a fair description of the *réunions*?
3 From the evidence in 5.6–5.8, summarise the motives which lay behind the search for *réunions*.
4 How can the policy of *réunions* be related to Louis's general objectives in foreign policy [5.1–5.3]?
5 How wise do you think the policy of *réunions* was? What possible dangers can you envisage ahead for Louis XIV?

Behind these *réunions* there lay a clear strategic purpose: to control certain key bridgeheads and fortresses which would protect France in the event of another war against the United Provinces and/or the Emperor. By far the most important of these were the mighty strongholds of Strasbourg and Luxembourg. Three times during the Dutch War, control of Strasbourg had allowed the Emperor's armies to march into Alsace. However, the *parlement* of Metz could find no evidence that the city was a French 'dependency' and Louis therefore resorted to military force. On 30 September 1681, 30,000 French troops occupied Strasbourg, so establishing a base from which Louis's armies could march straight towards Vienna. The Emperor protested bitterly, but the inhabitants of Strasbourg itself were remarkably acquiescent. The Marquis de Louvois reported to Louis on 4 October:

5.9

Monsieur de Montclar[1] this morning received the Mayor of Strasbourg's oath of loyalty, which he gave with very good grace. The people seem very happy indeed with the change of rule, and so far I have only received one complaint, from a woman whose husband got drunk with one of our soldiers . . . Your Majesty can rest assured, now that this citadel is taken, that we have a fortress with four   5
bastions as a bridgehead, and that no power in Europe will be in a position to drive Your Majesty out of this stronghold.

[1] 'Monsieur de Montclar' = the commander of Louis XIV's troops in Alsace.

The Marquis de Louvois to Louis XIV, 4 October 1681, in Camille Rousset,
Histoire de Louvois et de son administration politique et militaire **(4 vols.,
Paris, 1862–4), vol. III**

Although alarmed by these *réunions* along his frontiers, the Emperor was much too preoccupied with repelling Turkish invaders (who reached the gates of Vienna in July 1683) to take any military action against France. Louis, a close trading partner of the Turks, became the only major European ruler not to assist the Emperor. Instead, he pressed on with further *réunions* and – acting upon a decree by the *parlement* of Metz – demanded the imperial fortress of Luxembourg. When the Emperor refused, the Maréchal de Créqui besieged Luxembourg and took it on 4 June 1684. **5.10** shows both sides of a medal struck to commemorate this event. The obverse side [**5.10a**] bears Louis XIV's profile surrounded by an inscription proclaiming him the 'Most Christian King'; while on the reverse side [**5.10b**] a female figure symbolising Security reclines on a rock, which depicts the natural defences of Luxembourg. She holds a crown, and rests her arm on a shield bearing the arms of Luxembourg.

5.10

A   B

The inscriptions read:
(A) LUDOVICUS MAGNUS REX CHRISTIANISSIMUS [Louis the Great, Most Christian King]
(B) SECURITAS PROVINCIARUM. LUCEMBURGUM CAPTUM. M.DC.LXXXIV
     [The security of the provinces. Luxembourg captured, 1684]

Medal commemorating the capture of Luxembourg, viewed on both sides, 1684, in L'Académie Royale des Médailles et des Inscriptions, *Médailles sur les principaux événements du règne de Louis le Grand, avec des explications historiques* (Paris, 1702)

(;

The Emperor, still fighting the Turks, was simply not in a position to drive French troops out of Luxembourg. Instead, he signed the Truce of Ratisbon (15 August 1684) with Louis. This effectively 'froze' the boundaries between France, the Empire and the Low Countries for twenty years. Although these terms would prevent further *réunions*, Louis was allowed to keep all those areas which he had occupied so far. His policy of piecemeal annexation had apparently triumphed, and the poet and play-wright Jean Racine (1639–99) celebrated the new *pax gallicana*, a European order dominated by France.

But Racine crowed too soon. Despite the confirmation of all his gains at Ratisbon, Louis was still not satisfied, and in 1688 seized the Electorate of Cologne and the fortress of Philippsburg. Louis's neighbours finally decided that the time had come to form a coalition which would keep him within the frontiers established at Ratisbon. The Emperor, Great Britain, Spain, Savoy and several German principalities therefore signed the Grand Alliance of Vienna (12 May 1689). Louis's refusal to withdraw from Cologne and Philippsburg precipitated the Nine Years' War, a bitter conflict eventually settled in September 1697 by the Treaty of Ryswick. Perhaps the most important clauses of this treaty were those concerning *réunions* [5.11]. These permitted eighty-two towns, villages and hamlets in Alsace annexed since 1680 to remain within France. The only one of any size or strategic significance was Strasbourg. For all other *réunions* outside Alsace, the following principles applied:

5.11

X   . . . All . . . *réunions* . . . shall be completely . . . ended: hence all legal
proceedings, sentences, separations, incorporations, decrees, confiscations,
réunions, declarations, rulings, edicts and all acts whatsoever made in the
name of and on behalf of His Most Christian Majesty by reason of the said
réunions, whether by the *parlement* at Metz, or by the other courts of   5
justice . . . against His Catholic Majesty[1] and his subjects, and will be
revoked and annulled for ever, as if they had never been . . .

XI   All the places, towns, boroughs, villages and dependencies hereby returned
and ceded by His Most Christian Majesty, without reserving or returning any
of them, will revert to the possession of His Catholic Majesty, to be enjoyed   10
with all their rights, advantages, profits and revenues, with the same
boundaries, and the same rights of property, jurisdiction and sovereignty that
they enjoyed before the last war . . .

[1] 'His Catholic Majesty' = the title traditionally adopted by kings of Spain.

The Treaty of Ryswick, 20 September 1697, in *Les Grands Traités du Règne de Louis XIV*, ed. Henri Vast (3 vols., Paris, 1893–9), vol. II

Louis accepted the demands of the Treaty of Ryswick with remarkably good grace. He even ordered the Archbishop of Paris to hold a thanksgiving service in the cathedral of Notre-Dame. The French people, he explained, had good reason to rejoice at the peace terms [5.12].

5.12

The moment decreed by Heaven for the reconciliation of the nations has arrived; Europe is at peace. The ratification of the treaty which my ambassadors concluded recently with those of the Emperor and the Empire has put the seal on the re-establishment of this tranquillity which everyone has desired . . . Strasbourg, one of the principal ramparts of the Empire and of heresy, [is] united for ever with   5 the Church and my crown; the Rhine established as the barrier between France and Germany; . . . these are the gains of the recent treaty.

Louis XIV, *Lettre du Roy écrite à monseigneur l'archevêque de Paris pour faire chanter le* Te Deum *en l'église Notre-Dame, en action des grâces de la paix conclue avec l'Empereur et l'Empire* (Paris, 1698)

Questions

1   Explain and comment on the following phrases:
    (i)   'The security of the provinces' [5.10b]
    (ii) 'the Rhine established as the barrier between France and Germany' [5.12, lines 6–7].
2   What light does 5.9 throw on popular reactions to the annexation of Strasbourg? What might be the limitations of this source?
3   What may be gleaned from 5.10 about how the French government perceived and justified the policy of *réunions*?
4   Does 5.11 mark the final defeat of Louis's policy of *réunions*?
5   Do you find Louis's gloss [5.12] on the Treaty of Ryswick justified by the actual treaty [5.11]? Consider the implications of your answer.
6   What does 5.12 reveal about Louis's attitudes towards war and peace? Is this borne out by other evidence in this chapter, and elsewhere?
7   'A successful policy ruined by Louis's own insatiable greed.' Is this a fair description of the *réunions*?
8   From the material in this chapter, and your wider reading, how important was the policy of *réunions* in the long term?

But did Louis have an ulterior motive for his favourable response to the Treaty of Ryswick? Many historians have suggested that he wished to improve his international image in order to exploit an impending crisis over

5.13

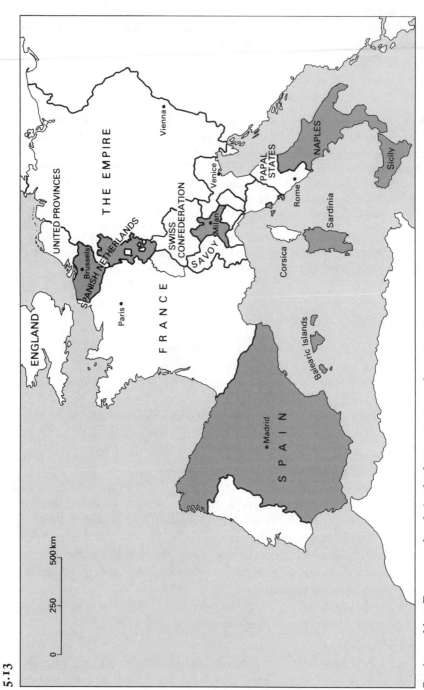

Spain and her European lands in the late seventeenth century

the Spanish succession. This brings us to our second case study of Louis's foreign policy in action. By the late 1690s, the sickly and feeble-minded King Charles II of Spain was not expected to live much longer. Unfortunately he had no children. That left three main contenders for the Spanish throne, each with a valid claim: Louis's own son (Charles II's nephew); Joseph Ferdinand, son of the Elector of Bavaria (his great-nephew); and the Archduke Charles, son of the Habsburg Emperor (another great-nephew). At stake was a vast inheritance consisting of Spain together with her European and American dominions. Map 5.13 shows the extent of Spanish territory within Europe alone.

It was an enormously tempting prize. But Louis realised that to assert French claims might well provoke another European conflict, something which he could ill afford in the aftermath of the Nine Years' War. He therefore sought a diplomatic solution, and in April 1698 instructed the Comte de Tallard, French ambassador in London, to discuss the possibility of partitioning Spain and her dominions with William III. Having just spent nine years fighting Louis, William refused to give much ground. Yet Louis was very reluctant to break off the negotiations. He explained why in a letter to Tallard on 15 July 1698 [5.14].

5.14

I have examined very carefully all the problems that one could foresee either by suspending the negotiations with the King of Great Britain or by concluding them. The first seems to me to be the greater [danger]. In breaking with [William III] we would indirectly force him to open talks with Bavaria, and the other princes of the Empire . . . It would be easy for him to win them over . . . [and] treaties could be   5 signed during his stay in Holland . . . With a league being formed [against France] before the death of the King of Spain, it would be impossible to support the legitimate rights of my son to this succession . . . without causing a new war in Europe as great as the last one.

Louis XIV to the Comte de Tallard, 15 July 1698, in A. Legrelle, *La diplomatie française et la succession d'Espagne* (6 vols., Paris, 1895–9) (hereafter cited as Legrelle), vol. II

The talks continued through the summer and autumn, and bore fruit in the First Partition Treaty, signed by representatives of France, Great Britain and the United Provinces on 11 October 1698 [5.15]. The main articles of this treaty were as follows:

5.15

2   The state of the King of Spain's health gives grounds for fearing that he does
    not have long to live . . . It is essential to make plans for the event of his death
    because the opening of the succession question would inevitably cause another
    war if [any of the three contenders] insisted upon his claim . . .

4   It has therefore been concluded and agreed that should the King of Spain   5
    die . . . without children . . . the Dauphin will have for his share, in full and
    rightful possession, and renouncing all his claims to the Spanish throne, . . .
    the kingdoms of Naples and Sicily, and the dependencies of Spain on the coast
    of Tuscany . . .

5   The said Crown of Spain and the other kingdoms, islands, states, countries   10
    and places which are currently dependent upon it, shall be given and assigned
    (except for what is mentioned in the previous article, which will form the
    Dauphin's share) to the eldest son of the Elector of Bavaria . . .

6   An exception to the above arrangements is made of the Duchy of Milan,
    which . . . shall be given to the Archduke Charles of Austria, second son of the   15
    Emperor Leopold, thereby extinguishing all the said Emperor's rights and
    claims . . .

The First Partition Treaty, 11 October 1698, in Legrelle vol. II

It seemed that careful diplomacy had produced a settlement acceptable to
all parties. But then, in February 1699, the young Prince Joseph Ferdinand
of Bavaria, who stood to inherit the bulk of Spanish lands, caught smallpox
and died. Again Europe faced the threat of war; and again Louis suggested
peace negotiations to William III. These talks proved much more difficult
and protracted than those in 1698. But eventually the Second Partition
Treaty [5.16] was signed by France and Great Britain on 13 March 1700,
and by the United Provinces on 25 March.

5.16

4   It has . . . been concluded and agreed that should the King of Spain die . . .
    without children . . . the Dauphin will have for his share, in full and rightful
    possession, and renouncing all his claims to the Spanish throne, . . . the
    kingdoms of Naples and Sicily, and the dependencies of Spain on the coast of
    Tuscany . . . Furthermore, the lands of the Duke of Lorraine . . . shall be   5
    ceded and conveyed to the Dauphin, his children, heirs and successors . . . in
    full and rightful possession, in place of the Duchy of Milan, which shall be
    ceded and conveyed in return to the Duke of Lorraine . . .

6   The Crown of Spain and the other kingdoms, islands, lands, countries and
    places which the Catholic King[1] currently possesses, both within and without   10
    Europe, shall be given and assigned to the Archduke Charles, second son of

the Emperor (except for what is mentioned in the previous article, which will form the Dauphin's share, and the Duchy of Milan, in conformity with the said article), in full and rightful possession . . .

¹ 'the Catholic King': see 5.11, note 1.

The Second Partition Treaty, 13/25 March 1700, in Legrelle vol. III

Questions

1 Does 5.14 mark a shift from Louis's earlier methods in foreign policy? Explain your answer.
2 Account for the differences between the First and Second Partition Treaties [5.15–5.16]. What features (if any) do they have in common?
3 From which of the two Partition Treaties [5.15–5.16] did France derive more benefit, and why?
4 Consider the strategic implications of each of the Partition Treaties [5.15–5.16] in the light of map 5.13. Which was more likely to achieve a stable settlement in Europe, and why?
5 'The pursuit of self-aggrandisement by diplomatic means.' From the evidence in 5.14–5.16, is this a fair description of Louis's motives?
6 How can Louis's approach to the Partition Treaties be related to his overall goals in foreign policy [5.1–5.3]?

At no stage in any of these negotiations did anyone bother to consult Spain. It hardly seemed necessary, for by the autumn of 1700 Charles II lay close to death. His doctors, perplexed by what were probably epileptic fits, thought him bewitched and summoned an exorcist. Yet the King bitterly resented the planned partition of his empire, and on 2 October was well enough to compose a will. Article thirteen of this lengthy document stated: 'I declare my successor to be . . . the Duke of Anjou, second son of [the] Dauphin; and as such, I call him to the succession in all my kingdoms and dominions, without exception of any part of them.' Charles II apparently believed that only a French prince – powerfully assisted by Louis XIV – could prevent the break-up of Spain. Thus when Charles died on 1 November, the whole Spanish inheritance fell into the lap of Louis XIV's grandson.

This placed Louis in an extraordinary dilemma. Should he stand by the Second Partition Treaty, which France had signed but which gave her very little territory; or should he accept Charles II's will and declare his grandson ruler of the entire Spanish Empire? After some hesitation he reached a decision, and summoned the Spanish ambassador to Versailles on 16 November. Philippe, Marquis de Dangeau (1638–1720), an urbane courtier and diarist who had made a fortune from gambling, takes up the story:

5.17

The King summoned the Spanish ambassador to his chamber, and then he called the Duke of Anjou, who was in the ante-chamber, and said to the ambassador: 'You may salute him as your king.' The ambassador went down on his knees and kissed his hand in the Spanish manner. The ambassador paid a long tribute in Spanish, and when he had finished the King said to him: 'He does not yet   5
understand Spanish; I will reply on his behalf'. The courtiers were waiting outside the King's chamber; His Majesty ordered the double doors to be opened and everyone to come in, and he said: 'Gentlemen, before you stands the King of Spain. His birth has called him to this crown; the whole nation wished it and asked me for it without delay, and I have granted it to them with pleasure. It is the   10
command of heaven.' Then, turning to the King of Spain, he said: 'Be a good Spaniard, that is now your first duty; but remember that you were born French and maintain the union between the two nations. That is the way to make them happy and to preserve the peace of Europe.'

Journal du Marquis de Dangeau, ed. M. Soulié *et al.* (19 vols. in 9, Paris, 1854–9), vol. VII

Philip V, as the Duke of Anjou became, left for Spain on 5 December, and reached Madrid the following February. The Spaniards were delighted with their new king; but the other European powers accused Louis of bad faith and formed a coalition to implement the Second Partition Treaty. Philip V refused to leave Spanish territory, and so on 7 September 1701 Great Britain, the United Provinces and the Habsburg Emperor signed a Grand Alliance [5.18] to enforce a French withdrawal.

5.18

[Louis XIV], aiming at the [Spanish] succession for his grandson the Duke of Anjou, and pretending a right did accrue to him by a certain will of the deceased King, has usurped the possession of the entire . . . Spanish monarchy for the aforesaid Duke of Anjou . . . The kingdoms of France and Spain are [now] so closely united and cemented that they may seem henceforward . . . as one and the   5
same kingdom . . . So it appears, unless timely care be taken, that His Imperial Majesty will be destitute of all hopes of ever receiving . . . the fiefs [= lands] belonging to [him] in Italy and the Spanish Netherlands . . . [and] that the French

and Spaniards, being thus united, will within a short time become so formidable to all that they may easily assume to themselves the dominion over all Europe. [The   10 Emperor, the King of Great Britain, and the United Provinces] have [therefore] thought a strict conjunction and alliance between themselves necessary for repelling the greatness of the common danger.

The Grand Alliance, 7 September 1701, in Charles Jenkinson, first Earl of Liverpool, *A Collection of all the treaties of peace, alliance, and commerce, between Great Britain and other powers, from ... 1648 ... to 1783* (3 vols., London, 1785), vol. I

So began the international warfare which the Partition Treaties had sought to prevent. The War of the Spanish Succession proved to be the most terrible of all Louis's conflicts, and lasted until within a year of his own death. France suffered a string of military defeats at the battles of Blenheim (1704), Ramillies (1706), Oudenarde (1708) and Malplaquet (1709). Eventually, peace treaties were signed at Utrecht (1713) and Rastatt (1714) which allowed Philip V to remain king of Spain and her American colonies, but ceded Spanish lands in the Netherlands and in Italy to the Emperor. France also lost several key strategic sites on her north-eastern frontier.

What had been gained through all this bloodshed? It is extremely difficult to draw up a balance-sheet for Louis XIV's foreign policy, to weigh up strategic benefits against the loss of life, revenue and property. Perhaps all we can do, in conclusion, is to compare the eastern frontier of France in 1661 [5.19a], when Louis assumed personal control of government, with that in 1715 [5.19b], the year of his death. These two maps will help you to decide for yourself just how much Louis's foreign policy had achieved.

5.19a

The eastern frontier of France in 1661

5.19b

The eastern frontier of France in 1715

Questions

1   Consider the arguments for and against Louis's behaviour as recounted in 5.17.

2   If you had been a senior adviser to Louis XIV in early November 1700, what course would you have urged him to take regarding the Spanish Succession, and why?

3   How far was 5.18 a just response to Louis's decision in 5.17? Give your reasons.

4   Was some kind of international conflict over the Spanish Succession inevitable? Explain your answer.

5   Which European power was most to blame for the outbreak of the War of the Spanish Succession, and why?

6   What may be learnt from maps 5.19a–b about the nature and achievements of Louis XIV's foreign policy? Does this confirm or conflict with other evidence which you have seen in this chapter and elsewhere?

7   In the light of this chapter as a whole, and your wider reading, did Louis XIV's foreign policy follow any consistent principles? If so, what were they? If not, in what ways did his foreign policy change over time?

8   Using the evidence in this chapter, and elsewhere, how successfully did Louis XIV achieve his foreign policy objectives [5.1–5.3]?

9   Turn back to documents 5.4–5.5. Have the two case studies of Louis XIV's foreign policy in action changed your opinion about the fairness of these attacks? Explain your answer.

10   From your wider knowledge of the period, how typical or untypical of Louis's foreign policy as a whole are these case studies of the *réunions* and the Partition Treaties?

11   Using materials in this book, and elsewhere, consider how far Louis's foreign policy reinforced or obstructed his policies in other areas.

6 Versailles: court and culture

One of the many ways in which Louis XIV served as a model for other crowned heads throughout Europe lay in his creation of a splendid, glittering Court. During his reign all the royal palaces, including the Louvre in Paris and Fontainebleau in the Loire valley, were restored and extended. But above all Louis XIV will always be remembered for the creation of the magnificent palace and park at Versailles near Paris. Louis XIII had built a relatively modest hunting lodge at Versailles in 1631–4. At that time, and during the early decades of Louis XIV's reign, the French Court was itinerant, moving from palace to palace throughout the year. But in 1671 Louis XIV decided to transform Versailles into a setting appropriate for the 'Sun-King'. He needed a palace close to Paris, but increasingly found the old Louvre in the city centre cramped and uncomfortable. Furthermore, he wished to show the world that French kings could build in the open countryside and had nothing to fear from their subjects. Versailles thus helped to affirm the monarchy's recovery after the Frondes, and in 1682 the royal Court was moved there permanently. This chapter is devoted entirely to the nature, significance and symbolism of Louis XIV's Court, especially during the years when it resided at Versailles. The first section explores the political functions of the Court, the ways in which it sought to enhance royal authority, and the contrasting impressions which it made on contemporaries. Then we will turn to the culture of the Court, and examine how the palace and gardens of Versailles, and the entertainments held within them, were designed to celebrate the rule of 'le Roi-Soleil'.

The politics of the Court

Perhaps the most important purpose of the Court was to provide a grandiose setting for the King and his family. This ambition was not motivated solely by royal vanity: the public display of the monarch against an appropriate backdrop also had a crucial role to play in political processes. In his *Mémoires* [6.1], Louis argued that it was essential for the monarch to be constantly visible and accessible to his subjects:

6.1

A prince, and a king of France, must see . . . public amusements as not so much our own as those of our Court and of all our people. There are some nations where the majesty of kings largely consists of not letting themselves be seen, and this may have its reasons among minds used to servitude, which can only be ruled by fear and terror; but this is not the nature of the French people, and as far back as our   5 histories go, if there is any feature unique to this monarchy, it is the free and easy access of the subjects to their prince. It is an equality of justice between him and them, which embraces them in a mild and honest harmony, despite their almost infinite difference in birth, rank and power. Experience has already shown that this system is good and useful for us, for in all past centuries there is no memory of any   10 empire having lasted as long as this one, and even now it does not seem about to fall.

Mémoires de Louis XIV

As a result, the King rarely enjoyed any privacy. Primi Visconti (see document 1.14) has left us the following account of a lifestyle governed by the need for public display, and lived out under under a constant spotlight:

6.2

In public, he is full of solemnity and very different from how he is as a private individual. When I am in his apartment with other courtiers, I have often noticed that if the door happens to be left open accidentally, or he is going out, he immediately composes himself and adopts another facial expression, as if he were to appear on stage; in short, he knows how to be the king in all things . . . There   5 are no intermediaries: if you want something, you must appeal directly to him and not to anyone else. He listens to everybody, receives memoranda, and always replies gracefully and majestically 'I will see', and everyone leaves satisfied . . . It is a wonderful sight to see him leave the château [= Versailles] with his bodyguards, his carriages, his horses, the courtiers, valets and a confused multitude of people   10 all . . . running noisily around him. It reminds me of a queen bee when she flies out into the fields with her swarm.

Primi Visconti, *Mémoires sur la cour de Louis XIV*, ed. J. Lemoine (Paris, 1908)

Every aspect of Louis's daily routine was conducted in the public gaze. In particular, the King's subjects were admitted into his bedchamber to watch him get up (the *lever*) and go to bed (the *coucher*). This was true even before the Court moved to Versailles. For instance, John Locke described how the King's day started on Wednesday 28 December 1678:

6.3

At the King's Lever [= getting up] which I saw this morning at St Germans,[1] there is nothing so remarkable as his great devotion which is very exemplary, for as soon as ever he is dressed, he goes to his bedside where he kneels down to his prayers, several priests kneeling by him, in which posture he continues for a pretty while, not being disturbed by the noise and buzz of the rest of the chamber, which   5 is full of people standing and talking one to another.

[1] 'St Germans' = the palace of St Germain-en-Laye, in Paris.

Locke's Travels

Questions

1   Explain and comment on the following phrases:
   (i)   'the free and easy access of the subjects to their prince' [**6.1, lines 6–7**]
   (ii)   'an equality of justice between him and them' [**6.1, lines 7–8**]
   (iii)   'as if he were to appear on stage' [**6.2, lines 4–5**].
2   'The King's life became a Court ceremony' (John B. Wolf). How far do **6.1–6.3** support this view?
3   From the evidence in **6.1–6.3**, what advantages did Louis XIV derive from being constantly accessible to his subjects?
4   Do **6.1–6.3** suggest that there were any disadvantages in this system? Explain your answer.
5   Do **6.1–6.3** imply any distinction between the King's public and private lives? What does your answer reveal about the nature of monarchy in this period?
6   From the material in **6.1–6.3**, and elsewhere, how important do you think public display was as an ingredient of Louis's political power?
7   From the evidence in this chapter so far, and your wider knowledge, how far did the office and the person of the king become identical under Louis XIV? Explain your answer.

It was not only the King who had to behave in a very formal, ceremonial manner. His courtiers were required to show deference and respect, and this served to enhance Louis's position even further. Here, for example, is how the contemporary writer and moralist Jean de La Bruyère (1639–96) described the behaviour of courtiers in the royal chapel at Versailles:

E

6.4

The courtiers . . . have both their God and their King: the great of the nation assemble every day, at a certain time, in a temple which they call a church. At the far end of this temple there is an altar consecrated to their God, where a priest celebrates the mysteries which they call holy, sacred and fearful. The great ones form a vast circle at the foot of this altar, and stand erect, their backs to the priests 5 and the sacred mysteries, and their faces raised towards their King, who is seen kneeling in a gallery, and on whom they appear to be concentrating with all their hearts and minds. One cannot help but see in this custom a kind of subordination; for these people appear to worship their prince while he in turn worships God.

Oeuvres complètes de La Bruyère, ed. J. Benda (Paris, 1934)

The self-conscious behaviour of the courtiers, and their contempt for the world outside, also made an impression on the historian César Vichard, Abbé de Saint-Réal (1639–92):

6.5

The people of the Court are like a foreign nation within the State, composed of people drawn from different places. They are not all people of intellect, but they nearly all have an admirable politeness instead. They are not all worthy people, but they do have an air and a manner which make one think they are. Their flexible and accommodating minds can adopt any stance on any matter, so that it is 5 impossible to know their true feelings. The contempt which they have for anything which is not of the Court is hard to imagine, and goes to the point of extravagance . . . But although they have very good taste, they mostly have very little learning, and they only appear knowledgeable on all sorts of things by a few well-turned phrases, and by the respect which makes everyone fall silent in their 10 presence.

Les Oeuvres de M. l'Abbé de Saint-Réal (8 vols., Paris, 1757), vol. II

Such deferential manners reflected the King's own exacting standards. He was very closely involved in the running of the Court, and took care to supervise the behaviour of his courtiers. A typical example was his deep hostility to duelling as a means of settling private quarrels, and in August 1679 Louis issued the first effective 'regulations for the suppression of the duel' in French history. His concern with the morality of the Court also emerges in other sources. The next two extracts [6.6–6.7] are taken from another contemporary account of the Court, written by Ezéchiel Spanheim (1629–1710), who served as envoy to France from several German princes in 1666, 1668 and 1678–87. During his last embassy, undertaken for the

Elector of Brandenburg-Prussia, Spanheim described Louis's careful management of the Court:

6.6

He likes order, deference and sobriety . . . [and] as a result has a well-regulated Court and submissive courtiers. He knows how to distance [the Court] from vices which were only too common there – quarrels, debauchery, impiety, profligacy, and irreverence in the worship of God. He has also declared openly against the flagrant vices of the younger courtiers and the disgraceful conduct of his own   5 children, and he has not spared from punishment or correction those who are suspected or convicted of misbehaviour, such as the Duc de Vermandois, the son of the King and Madame de la Vallière,[1] and the Prince de Conti, a prince of the blood. Thus one cannot deny that the King is naturally an enemy of vice, except perhaps when he is carried away by his temperament and by bad examples . . . His   10 conduct is as regular and uniform in amusements as in public affairs, and thus he does not dissipate or forget himself in the former or become too lax in the latter.

[1] 'Madame de la Vallière' = the first of Louis XIV's mistresses.

Ezéchiel Spanheim, *Relation de la Cour de France en 1690*, ed. Emile Bourgeois (Paris, 1900) (hereafter cited as Spanheim, *Relation*)

But, following the classical conventions of portraiture so fashionable in the late seventeenth century, Spanheim then turned to the less praiseworthy aspects of Louis's character and Court [6.7]. In particular, he contrasted the extravagance of Versailles with the widespread poverty in France as a whole.

6.7

As [Louis] is more concerned to have his people regard him as a master than as a father, his reward is their submission and their dependence rather than their affection. He is not motivated by a genuine desire to relieve their miseries. Thus, it may be said that if he loves to give, he loves even more to save; that his kindness or generosity is usually motivated by self-interest; that he gives as much or more by   5 ostentation as by choice. Thus, he is the friend both of splendour and of economy . . . One need only reflect, on the one hand, on the eighty million [*livres*] which the palace, gardens and fountains of Versailles cost him, [or] on the work begun on Madame de Maintenon's[1] aqueduct, where more than 30,000 men worked for three years to direct, from a distance of sixteen French leagues, the   10 water of a river into the reservoirs of Versailles; and on the other hand, on the misery of the common people and the peasants, exhausted by the *tailles*,[2] by having to lodge soldiers, and by the *gabelles*.[3]

[1] 'Madame de Maintenon' = Louis XIV's second wife.
[2] '*tailles*' = a direct tax, like a land tax.
[3] '*gabelles*' = a tax on salt.

Spanheim, *Relation*

The final extract in this section [**6.8**] comes (like documents **1.15** and **3.4**) from the *Mémoires* of the Duc de Saint-Simon. Never one to mince words, Saint-Simon had this to say about the palace and gardens of Versailles:

6.8

Versailles [is] the gloomiest and most unpleasant of all places, without a view, without any woods, without any water, for the ground there is all quicksand or marsh, and the air is bad as a result. [The King] liked to tyrannise nature, to subjugate it by art and treasure. Without following any general design, he built the beautiful and the ugly, the vast and the narrow, one after the other, all jumbled   5
together. His apartment and that of the Queen are the last word in inconvenience, with views of closets, dull, cramped and stinking. The gardens, which are magnificent to behold but disgusting to use, are also in bad taste . . . The violence which has been done to nature everywhere repels and disgusts. The abundance of water, forced up and channelled from all directions, is made green, thick and   10
muddy; it spreads an unhealthy and perceptible humidity, [and] an odour which is even worse . . . I might never finish talking about the monstrous defects of a palace so immense and so costly, with its trappings, which are even more so.

***Mémoires de Saint-Simon* vol. XXVIII**

Questions

1 Explain and comment on the following phrases:
   (i) 'these people appear to worship their prince' [**6.4, line 9**]
   (ii) '[Louis] is more concerned to have his people regard him as a master than as a father' [**6.7, lines 1–2**].
2 Louis XIV 'had successfully domesticated his nobles' (J. Levron). To what extent do **6.4–6.5** bear out this statement?
3 According to Spanheim, what were Louis's aims in his running of the Court [**6.6–6.7**]?
4 What evidence for and against Spanheim's claims in **6.7** have you found elsewhere in this book?
5 Comment on the tone of **6.8**.

6   Do you think that Saint-Simon's charges in **6.8** are fair? Explain your answer.

7   From the evidence presented in this chapter so far, what political purposes did the Court serve? Justify your response.

8   Looking back over earlier chapters, could Louis have achieved the same degree of control in other areas had he not possessed this kind of Court?

The culture of the Court

We now turn from political themes to the cultural aspects of the Court. The palace, furnishings and gardens of Versailles were explicitly designed to glorify and celebrate the King's achievements. Louis employed the same team which had created Vaux-le-Vicomte for Fouquet: the château was designed by Louis Le Vau and its interior filled with paintings by Charles Le Brun, while the vast gardens were laid out by André Le Nôtre. After Le Vau's death in 1670, Jules Hardouin Mansart took over as the chief architect. The sheer size of the monument which they created was remarkable. A contemporary painting by Pierre Patel [**6.9**] provides a bird's-eye view of the original hunting-lodge as it looked in 1668. By contrast, a modern aerial view [**6.10**] shows the scale of the changes which took place under Louis XIV.

6.9   Pierre Patel, *View of Versailles*, 1668

6.10

Aerial view of the palace and gardens of Versailles today

The interior of the palace was likewise conceived on an heroic scale. The most spectacular room of all was the famous Hall of Mirrors ('Galerie des Glaces') [6.11], which measured 239 by 34 feet, and had a ceiling adorned with paintings by Le Brun.

6.11

The Hall of Mirrors, Versailles, 1678–85

Le Brun's panels on the ceiling celebrated episodes from Louis's life and career. Painting **6.12** was one of the most richly symbolic. Entitled 'The King rules by himself' ('Le Roi gouverne par lui-même'), it depicted Louis's assumption of personal control of French government in 1661. Louis is portrayed in Roman armour (but wearing the French king's mantle), and is being guided by Minerva (representing wisdom). Below are scenes of joy in the King's rule; while the storm clouds overhead represent Louis's foreign enemies.

6.12

Charles Le Brun, *The King Rules by Himself*, c. 1681

The Hall of Mirrors was not the only immense room within the palace. The visitor would pass through a series of state apartments named after classical gods, goddesses and heroes: the Salon of Diana (a billiard room); the Salon of Venus (a reception room); and the Salon of Mars (a ballroom). Finally, he or she would reach the inner apartments of the King and

Queen: the Salon of Mercury (the state bedchamber); and the Salon of Apollo (the throne room). Louis's bedchamber [**6.13**] was specially designed to accommodate the large crowds which flocked daily to witness his *lever* and *coucher*.

6.13

The King's Bedchamber, Versailles, 1670–3

Questions

1   What can be learnt about the development of Versailles from the two views shown in **6.9–6.10**? Comment on the value of this sort of evidence to the historian.
2   What image of kingship does the Hall of Mirrors [**6.11**] convey?
3   Look at painting **6.12** and consider the significance of the following:
    (i)   the depiction of the King in Roman armour
    (ii) the French king's mantle which Louis is wearing
    (iii) the figure of Minerva
    (iv) the scenes of joy below
    (v)   the storm clouds overhead.

4   In plate **6.13** explain the significance of the following:
    (i)   the bed and its canopy
    (ii) the design above the bed
    (iii) the rail in front of the bed.
5   In what ways does the interior of Versailles [**6.9–6.13**] confirm or refute claims made about the Court in **6.1–6.8**? Explain your answer.
6   To what extent do **6.9–6.13** express notions of 'absolutism'? Explore the implications of your answer.

The official entertainments held at Versailles lived up to their magnificent setting. Particularly splendid were the royal ballets performed several times a year. Louis was a very keen participant, and regularly appeared in roles which portrayed him as a classical god. For example, in 1653 he took the part of Apollo in the spectacular finale of Isaac de Benserade's *Ballet of the Night (Ballet de la Nuit)*. The scenario for this finale ran as follows:

6.14

Dawn pulls a superb [= proud] chariot bringing the most beautiful sun [= Apollo] that one had ever seen; which at first dissipated the clouds, and then promised the most beautiful and the greatest day of the world.

***Les Oeuvres de Monsieur de Benserade*, ed. Charles de Sercy (2 vols., Paris, 1698), vol. II**

For his role as Apollo, Louis appeared for the first time in the dazzling clothes of the rising sun. This costume [**6.15**] was designed by Henry de Gissey and inaugurated the image of Louis as the 'Sun-King' which was to endure for the rest of his life.

6.15

Costume design for Louis XIV as Apollo, Henry de Gissey, 1653

Louis realised that such ballets played an important part in creating and glorifying his heroic royal persona. In 1663 he therefore founded an Academy of Dance which ensured that such entertainments were conducted regularly and professionally. This decision, and the political considerations which prompted it, formed the subject of one of Jean Loret's letters in verse to the Duchesse de Nemours:

6.16

The King does not cease to cherish
The beautiful arts that he made to flourish
In his kingdom of France;
He recognised especially the dance
Which gives grace and politeness   5
To both people and nobility.

It is a hundred times more charming
Than tournaments and combating,
Which even as symbols so grand
Only upset the peace of the land.   10
In their place, balls and ballets,
Either serious or diverting,
Make the fruits of peace alluring;
To achieve all this His Majesty,
By virtue of his supreme authority,   15
Has created the Academy of Dance.

Jean Loret, letter in verse to the Duchesse de Nemours, 1663, in *La Muze Historique, ou Recueil des Lettres en Vers . . . par Jean Loret*, ed. C.-L. Livet (4 vols., Paris, 1857–78), vol. IV

Questions

1   Why do you think that Louis was cast as Apollo in the *Ballet of the Night* [6.14–6.15]?
2   What seems to be the political message of 6.14?
3   Comment on the visual impact of 6.15.
4   What reasons are given in 6.16 for the King's creation of the Academy of Dance?
5   Assess the value as royal propaganda of entertainments such as the *Ballet of the Night*.
6   Using your wider knowledge, consider the political implications of the title 'Sun-King'. How far do you think Louis lived up to them?

The same glorification of the monarch was evident when the visitor stepped outside into the gardens of Versailles. These provided an opportunity for the 'Sun-King' to demonstrate his power over the natural landscape. Louis even wrote his own *Guide to the Display of the Gardens at Versailles (Manière de montrer les jardins de Versailles)* in the 1690s. This laid out a route taken by many visiting foreign dignitaries during the remainder of Louis's reign, and which the tourist can still follow today. Throughout the gardens, as inside the palace, Louis was depicted in heroic and glorious postures. One of the most splendid statues was Bernini's *Louis XIV Equestrian* [**6.17**], which portrayed Louis as the Roman hero Marcus Curtius. It was sculpted between 1671 and 1677, and placed at Versailles in 1685.

6.17

Gianlorenzo Bernini, *Louis XIV Equestrian*, 1671–7

Bernini's statue in turn inspired a series of poems and verses. **6.18** is taken from one of the most lavish, an anonymous poem which appeared in the official newspaper *Mercure Galant* in February 1686:

6.18

We see one who has never had an equal.
With a proud and daring air we see that animal
Rush forth furiously as if he wanted to split
One hundred thick battalions, in order to teach them
That everyone must yield to his royal burden.   5
. . . He traverses the seas to speedily carry
Louis the Great to the Mountain of Glory.

Part of an anonymous sonnet on Bernini's *Louis XIV Equestrian*, published in the *Mercure Galant* in February 1686

The theme of Apollo also appeared throughout the gardens. The most dramatic portrayal was Jean-Baptiste Tuby's fountain depicting Apollo in his sun-chariot leaving his home of Tethys (the sea) at daybreak [**6.19**]. This group, which was constructed in 1668–71, was intended to symbolise Louis's *lever*, when he rose and prepared for another busy day pursuing the policies explored in this book.

6.19

Jean-Baptiste Tuby, *Apollo Fountain*, 1668–71

Questions

1 What image of Louis XIV is presented in **6.17**?
2 Comment on the language of **6.18**.
3 Comment on the symbolism of the *Apollo Fountain* [**6.19**].
4 How are aspects of the gardens at Versailles [**6.17–6.19**] related to royal entertainments [**6.14–6.16**] and to the interior of the palace [**6.11–6.13**]? Explain your answer.
5 Discuss the following two assessments of the palace and gardens of Versailles in the light of the evidence presented in this chapter:
    (i)   'the supreme expression of Louis XIV's vision of kingship'
    (ii) 'a monstrous waste of national resources, in very bad taste'.
6 Is there any evidence in this chapter that worship of the King came to resemble a religion during Louis XIV's reign? Give reasons for your answer.
7 From the material in this chapter, and your wider knowledge, how far did the political and cultural aspects of the Court reinforce each other?
8 To what extent did the Court and culture of Versailles strengthen or weaken Louis's other policies, examined in earlier chapters? Explain your answer.
9 'An essential part of any absolutist régime.' Is this a fair comment on the role of the Court in Louis XIV's France, and in any other seventeenth-century European states which you have studied?

7 Assessment: historians on Louis XIV

So far in this book we have looked mainly at materials generated during Louis XIV's own lifetime: at his *Mémoires* and letters; at the descriptions of his contemporaries; at administrative documents; at pamphlets and tracts; and at buildings, medals and works of art. The aim of this final chapter is rather different. It is devoted entirely to the opinions of twentieth-century scholars. The ten extracts have been chosen to illustrate the very diverse ways in which historians have evaluated Louis and his reign. They are grouped around three themes. The first three all consider Louis's character and policies: what did he want, and how successful was he in achieving it? Then follow four extracts which discuss the nature of Louis's régime and offer contrasting views on how far this was an 'absolutist' state. The last three extracts assess Louis's impact and legacy. They discuss the nature of his achievements and the extent to which these died with him.

We begin, then, by focusing on Louis the man and the politician. In 7.1, Robin Briggs analyses the ways in which Louis's own personality helped to enhance the powers of the French monarchy. 7.2, written by John B. Wolf, considers the criteria by which we should judge Louis, and tries to set his 'aspirations' in the context of the values of his time. This group of documents concludes with an extract from what François Bluche called his 'sketch of a portrait' of Louis XIV [7.3].

7.1

[Under Louis XIV], free at last from overriding military needs, the monarchy could turn back to the policies of grandeur and internal reform foreshadowed by Richelieu more than three decades before. Much of this would certainly have occurred under any but the most incompetent king, yet Louis XIV's personality gave additional impetus to the assertion of royal power. A mediocre enough man in   5 many respects, the King had two great attributes: enormous physical vitality and an exceptionally strong will. His conventionality and intellectual limitation often turned to his advantage, helping him to play the role expected of him without any apparent doubt or hesitation. Above all, he found gratification not only in women,

gambling, and war, but in the painstaking everyday exercise of power, through the   10
bureaucratic institutions of his council. Confronted by a king whose will to rule
proved implacable, and who really worked at the job, such groups or style of
opposition as had survived the onslaught of the Cardinal-Ministers were quickly
swept aside. After the chaotic and complex story of the previous reigns, the
personal rule of Louis XIV seems almost devoid of dramatic events, a long era of   15
stability, even dullness.

Robin Briggs, *Early Modern France, 1560–1715* **(Oxford University Press,
Oxford, 1977)**

7.2

It is . . . impossible to sum up a career like that of Louis XIV in a few pages . . .
If we judge him by twentieth-century standards or test his politics by liberal-
democratic or communistic mystiques, Louis XIV and his ministers will often
appear arbitrary, arrogant, brutal, and many more such things; but neither Louis
XIV nor his ministers had any idea of these mystiques. They lived in a world that   5
was still theocentric, still dominated by God and directed by His interests. They
understood that God had created society and it did not occur to them to question
whether or not there were accompanying injustices. Indeed, to raise the issue
would presume to judge God's intentions in the creation of the world. But, like
other 'enlightened' men of his era, Louis XIV assumed that there was harmony in   10
the hierarchies of society; he warned his son to protect his subjects in the third
estate (bourgeoisie, artisans and peasants) as well as to respect the clergy and the
nobility. He also recommended to his successor a policy of peace with his
neighbours, though even when disaster followed his armies, Louis XIV believed
that his 'aspirations' were legitimate. He lived in a world that had not yet heard the   15
words 'humanitarian', 'cosmopolitan', 'liberal', 'democratic', 'socialist', and a host
of others associated with the earth-centred civilisation that was to follow.

Louis XIV: A Profile, **ed. John B. Wolf (Macmillan, London, 1972)**

7.3

This King, with so long a reign, and who seems to have given so much of himself
to the public, remains little known. Three centuries later, his intelligence is still
being debated. There is no agreement over any aspect of his character. The black
legend is partly responsible for this: it is certain that Fénelon, Father Jurieu and
the Duc de Saint-Simon continue to influence the posthumous judgements of our   5
countrymen. But also this fault condemned by Mr Michel Déon: our failure to
recognise true greatness . . . How would a prince of mediocre intelligence have
made so many short speeches, sober, precise, spiritual, concise and always
effective, in which we look in vain for traces of authoritarianism, arrogance, vanity
and banality? . . . How would a prince of mediocre intelligence have shown almost   10
infallible taste in matters of literature, architecture, painting, sculpture and music?

How would a prince of mediocre intelligence have known how to create both a
political style and an artistic style, to choose the best ministers and the best poets,
the best administrators and the best artists? . . . But if the thought of such a
remarkable character and such a great achievement were not enough to convince   15
us of the mind of this King, let us use . . . the argument of authority. Madame de
La Fayette, who sees in Louis XIV 'one of the greatest kings who has ever lived,
one of the most honest men in his kingdom' and almost 'the most perfect', only
holds one thing against him, the discretion which makes him too 'stingy with the
mind which heaven has given him'. The Abbé de Choisy, one of the finest minds   20
of his time, calls Louis 'an extraordinary genius'. Finally, Leibniz . . . speaks of the
'high intelligence' of this prince, 'one of the greatest kings of all time'.

François Bluche, *Louis XIV* (Arthème Fayard, Paris, 1986)

Questions

1 'A king whose will to rule proved implacable' [**7.1, lines 11–12**]. Do
   you agree?

2 Do **7.1–7.3** present a common picture of Louis XIV's personality? If so,
   what is it? If not, in what ways do they differ?

3 Do you think that **7.2** sets out the right criteria by which we should
   judge Louis's character and motives? Justify your response.

4 How persuasive do you find the arguments advanced in **7.1–7.3**?
   Explain your answer.

5 What evidence for and against the views advanced in **7.1–7.3** have you
   encountered in this book, and in your wider reading?

The next four extracts [**7.4–7.7**] all discuss the nature of Louis XIV's
régime. In **7.4**, Donald Pennington tells 'a story . . . of mitigated disaster',
in which he offsets Louis's policies against their heavy cost to French
society. **7.5**, by Thomas Munck, argues that Louis's primary concern was
foreign policy, and that he failed to carry out major institutional reforms
within France. Roger Mettam suggests in **7.6** that Louis faced exactly the
same problems as other early modern French monarchs, particularly the
difficulty of devising and pursuing effective policies in a country so vast and
diverse as France. Finally, in **7.7** John Miller analyses the formidable
structural obstacles which confronted Louis, and argues that these prevented the creation of a genuinely 'absolutist' régime.

7.4

The reign of Louis XIV has generally been regarded as the epitome of royal
absolutism in the seventeenth century. It is a story, like so many others, of
mitigated disaster. To give its tragic elements the firm structure approved by the
dramatists of his time, Louis would have needed to destroy himself amid the ruin
of his state. Instead he lived to see slow deterioration and indecisive defeat. It was   5
never apparent to him that the cost of the state, its monarchy, and its wars
impoverished the country, still less that in the long run a state identified with too
narrow a privileged élite would collapse. But he could hardly fail to see that the
glory he so assiduously manufactured lost its magic.

**D. H. Pennington, *Europe in the Seventeenth Century* (2nd edition,
Longman, Harlow, 1989)**

7.5

The show that Louis XIV made . . . of taking up full authority and responsibility in
March 1661, after the death of Cardinal Mazarin, was not as significant in practice
as it was meant to appear. Louis XIII had taken a central if less ostentatious role in
daily government . . . Louis XIV was a good judge of men, and indisputably
conscientious in terms of what he perceived to be his duties as monarch. Genuine   5
centralisation in the decision-making process was achieved through the use of the
very select inner council, the *conseil d'en haut*, whose membership never exceeded
half a dozen. But Louis's personal interests (like those of most rulers of the day)
lay primarily in the fields of diplomacy, international relations and war – the
protection of the royal patrimony in terms of prestige and European power – rather   10
than in the details of internal policy. He had neither the particular intelligence nor
the foresight or predisposition to perceive the need for deeper structural changes
of the kind that might have averted some of the problems of later years. Where
institutional traditions were altered, there was often an obvious and pragmatic
reason for doing so . . . None of the courts was actually restructured at any stage   15
until the late eighteenth century, and their judicial functions were left largely
intact: here, as with the provincial Estates and other traditional bodies, the
hallmark of French absolutism was conservation and adaptation to gradually
changing needs.

**Thomas Munck, *Seventeenth-Century Europe: State, Conflict and the
Social Order in Europe, 1598–1700* (Macmillan, London, 1990)**

7.6

Louis XIV [was] conservative by temperament as well as through circumstance.
Although he re-structured the policy-making machinery at the centre, he did not
make many changes in the personnel of the government nor in the group of
aristocratic advisers on whom the Crown had relied heavily in the years before
1661. Even in the prerogative areas of royal power he took careful account of   5

powerful vested interests, not wishing to alienate men who, if they were treated
honourably, would serve him well . . . Yet, despite the best intentions of the King
and his ministers, his government was soon to be a focus for much criticism and
discontent, especially when the problems of war returned to plague it. The
principal reason is a familiar one to historians of early modern France. Many   10
ministerial initiatives . . . seemed eminently sensible at Court where royal advisers
were considering the whole range of domestic and international issues which
currently affected the realm. In the provinces . . . such actions by a distant central
government not only offered no benefit but often savoured of . . . arbitrary
interference . . . France was a collection of very different provinces, many of which 15
had little in common. It was therefore almost impossible to devise a policy which
was in the best interests of the whole kingdom.

**Roger Mettam, *Power and Faction in Louis XIV's France* (Basil Blackwell,
Oxford, 1988)**

7·7

Some of the aims of [Louis XIV's] government were beyond the capabilities of any
seventeenth-century régime, especially those concerned with improving the
economy. But there were other structural weaknesses at least as intractable as the
problems imposed by distance and poor communications. First, Louis XIV never
began to unravel the tangle of institutions and jurisdictions which he had inherited. 5
He, his ministers and his *intendants* sought to manage the existing system, not to
change it. There remained innumerable problems of competing jurisdictions,
which the crown could exploit by setting one against another, but which also
involved officials and litigants in a huge expense of time and money. Second, the
more decision–making was concentrated in the King and at Versailles, the slower   10
it became. There was simply too much business, the wheels of government ground
slowly and the very thoroughness of the King and his councils made matters
slower still . . . French absolutism also suffered from two other major structural
weaknesses. One was venality of office. French kings had long raised money by
selling offices, a form of disguised borrowing . . . Successive ministers were well   15
aware of the problems created by venality, but it continued to grow. It represented
an accumulated debt upon which the crown could not renege . . . The continuing
growth of venality was a sign of French absolutism's second structural weakness:
the incompatibility of war and domestic reform. To rationalise and streamline the
administration . . . peace was essential . . . Every war brought a rash of new taxes   20
and offices . . . The net result was that the crown was left with an ever more
unwieldy administration and an ever greater burden of debt.

**John Miller, 'Introduction', in *Absolutism in Seventeenth-Century Europe*,
ed. John Miller (Macmillan, London, 1990)**

Questions

1   A 'story . . . of mitigated disaster' [**7.4, lines 2–3**]. How persuasive do you find Donald Pennington's verdict on the reign of Louis XIV, and why?
2   What steps towards the establishment of royal 'absolutism' are identified in **7.4–7.7**?
3   What obstacles to the establishment of royal 'absolutism' are identified in **7.4–7.7**?
4   Do **7.4–7.7** present a common view of the nature of Louis XIV's régime? If so, what is it? If not, in what ways do they differ?
5   What evidence for and against the views expressed in **7.4–7.7** have you found in this book, and elsewhere?
6   'Absolutism in seventeenth-century France was an impossible ideal.' Discuss with reference to **7.4–7.7** and your wider reading.

The final group of extracts presents different perspectives on Louis's achievements. In **7.8** Roger Lockyer weighs up Louis's 'considerable' achievement against the 'high' price which he – and France – paid for it. **7.9**, by J. H. Shennan, considers the many dimensions of Louis's impact both at home and abroad; while in **7.10**, John Morrill places Louis's career within the context of developments in French kingship during the seventeenth century as a whole.

7.8

The long War of the Spanish Succession had lowered Louis XIV's reputation at home and abroad and left the royal finances in a far worse state than they had been at his accession . . . It is not possible, of course, to strike a balance between French expenditure in men and money on the one hand and French gains in territory and general security on the other. Yet Louis's achievement was considerable. He gave   5
France much stronger frontiers in the north and east; he secured part of the great Spanish inheritance for his own Bourbon family; and he held the reviving power of the Austrian Habsburgs in check. He also prevented the modification of the treaty settlement of Westphalia in ways that might have been detrimental to French interests, and by constantly claiming more than he needed he retained more than   10
might otherwise have been the case. There was an element of the confidence-trickster about Louis, and he frequently overplayed his hand, but he left France firmly established among the great powers of Europe and French culture predominant throughout the entire continent. The price paid for this was high, perhaps too high, but Louis shared the prevailing assumption that money must   15
serve the demands of policy, not dictate it. Oblivious to the sufferings of his

subjects, he made *La Gloire* his objective and pursued it with such determination that he dazzled his contemporaries and established at least a claim to greatness.

Roger Lockyer, *Habsburg and Bourbon Europe, 1470–1720* (Longman, Harlow, 1974)

7.9

Louis XIV bequeathed a troubled inheritance to his great-grandson, Louis XV . . . He had done little to modernise the outmoded fiscal system or to loosen the straitjacket of social conservatism, and France would suffer increasingly during the eighteenth century from a lack of flexibility in both these areas. In addition, the religious controversy stirred up by the King's support for the papal Bull *Unigenitus*   5 would rage on for half a century after 1715. The King's reputation declined steadily both at home and abroad from the triumphant times of the early 1680s down to his death in 1715 . . . The King himself came to recognise that war had played too great a part in his reign, imposing suffering and hardship upon his own subjects and spreading fear amongst his neighbours. It is partly because he left   10 such a deep impression upon Europe that almost three and a half centuries after his accession he continues to attract the attention of historians. Louis also worked hard at creating his own legend. He understood the importance of political propaganda and we can still see the medals, the statues, the portraits and the palaces which embellished his reign and kept his reputation fresh . . . Under his   15 aegis France became the cultural leader of Europe and foreign princes flattered the King by building palaces in imitation of Versailles. Louis was one of the architects of modern France. His rule was more professional than that of any of his predecessors. He presided over an emerging state machine which would give far greater powers to central government than any dynastic ruler had ever achieved.   20 He also established the shape of France as we know it today. In other words, he achieved secure frontiers . . . He was fortunate to maintain those frontiers at Utrecht. Yet the fact that they still mark France's boundaries to the east is testimony to the significance of Louis XIV's achievement.

J.H. Shennan, *Louis XIV* (Methuen, London, 1986)

7.10

The achievements of French absolutism must not be ignored. In the course of the seventeenth century the monarchy extinguished all other patrimonies and ancient principalities within the bounds of the kingdom. Louis XIII and Louis XIV ruled as kings of France, not as king here, duke there. Their writs, the same writs, ran everywhere . . . The seventeenth century witnessed the creation of a common   5 coinage throughout France and the sponsorship of linguistic unity and purity. The Crown's legislative autonomy was acknowledged (in the sense of making law . . .). The king asserted (though this was periodically challenged) complete freedom to choose his own ministers, advisers, judges . . . The king's claim to be the source of

all justice was greatly strengthened. His ability to tax at will, or at least within the   10
limits of practical prudence, his ability to sustain a large standing army (and, as the
century wore on, to monopolise coercive power) and his growing control of the
Church in France, most obviously through the restoration of religious unity with
the revocation of the Edict of Nantes, more subtly through his rights within the
Church, and sponsorship of the Catholic reformation, are all extensions of   15
inherent strengths of the monarchy.

J. S. Morrill, 'French Absolutism as Limited Monarchy', *Historical Journal*
XXI (1978)

Questions

1   Do 7.8–7.10 present a common view of:
    (i)   Louis XIV's achievements during his own lifetime
    (ii) the extent to which these achievements survived him?
    If so, what do they agree about? If not, in what ways do they differ?
2   What evidence for and against the views of Louis XIV expressed in
    7.8–7.10 have you encountered in this book, and elsewhere?
3   What do the ten extracts in this chapter agree about? What do they
    disagree about?
4   From the evidence in this book as a whole, and your wider reading,
    what do you think was:
    (i)   Louis XIV's greatest achievement
    (ii) Louis XIV's greatest failure?
5   Using the materials in this book, and elsewhere, write your own brief
    (about 300 words) assessment of Louis XIV's career.

Bibliography

This Bibliography is divided into two parts. The first gives details of some general works relating to Louis XIV's life and times. It lists a selection of bibliographies, biographies, surveys, collections of essays and editions of source material. The second part contains some more specialised books and articles which illuminate particular themes. These items are arranged under the relevant chapter heading. Throughout I have confined myself exclusively to works in English.

General works

Bibliographies

There is a vast literature on Louis XIV's life and career. Three bibliographical articles offer particularly helpful guides to twentieth-century writings: John C. Rule, 'Louis XIV: a Bibliographical Introduction', in *Louis XIV and the Craft of Kingship*, ed. John C. Rule (Ohio, 1969), pp. 407–62; John B. Wolf, 'The Reign of Louis XIV: A Selected Bibliography of Writing since the War of 1914–1918', *Journal of Modern History* XXXVI (1964), 127–44; Ragnhild Hatton, 'Louis XIV: Recent Gains in Historical Knowledge', *Journal of Modern History* XLV (1973), 277–91.

For more recent works, see Mark Greengrass, 'Bibliographical Note', in his translation of François Bluche, *Louis XIV* (Oxford, 1990), pp. 649–51; and the relevant sections of the Historical Association's *Annual Bulletin of Historical Literature* (London, 1918–).

Biographies

There are innumerable biographies of Louis XIV, in many languages. Of those available in English, by far the best are:
    John B. Wolf, *Louis XIV* (London, 1968)
    François Bluche, *Louis XIV*, trans. M. Greengrass (Oxford, 1990)

Surveys

The following surveys, listed in alphabetical order, all provide excellent introductions to Louis XIV's career and to French history during his lifetime:

Jeremy Black, *Eighteenth-Century Europe, 1700–1789* (London, 1990)

Robin Briggs, *Early Modern France, 1560–1715* (Oxford, 1977), chapter 3(iv)

Roger Lockyer, *Habsburg and Bourbon Europe, 1470–1720* (Harlow, 1974), chapter 26

John Lough, 'France under Louis XIV', in *The New Cambridge Modern History*, vol. V, ed. F.L. Carsten (Cambridge, 1961), pp. 222–47

Roland Mousnier, *Louis XIV* (Historical Association pamphlet G.83, London, 1973)

Thomas Munck, *Seventeenth-Century Europe: State, Conflict and the Social Order in Europe, 1598–1700* (London, 1990), chapters 11–12

D. H. Pennington, *Europe in the Seventeenth Century* (2nd edition, Harlow, 1989), chapter 19

J. H. Shennan, *Louis XIV* (London, 1986)

Collections of essays

The following collections contain many valuable essays on various aspects of Louis's life and career:

Louis XIV and Absolutism, ed. Ragnhild Hatton (London, 1976)

Louis XIV and Europe, ed. Ragnhild Hatton (London, 1976)

William III and Louis XIV: essays 1680–1720, by and for Mark A. Thomson, ed. Ragnhild Hatton and J.S. Bromley (Liverpool, 1968)

State and Society in Seventeenth-Century France, ed. Raymond F. Kierstead (New York, 1975)

Louis XIV and the Craft of Kingship, ed. John C. Rule (Ohio, 1969)

Those essays which are especially relevant to particular chapters of this book are listed in the appropriate sections below.

Sources

Louis's own *Mémoires* are available in an English translation: *Louis XIV, Memoirs for the Instruction of the Dauphin*, trans. P. Sonnino (London, 1971). *Government and Society in Louis XIV's France*, ed. Roger Mettam (London, 1977) contains many important administrative documents which shed light on the ambitions and limitations of the régime; while the views of a wide variety of Louis XIV's contemporaries are presented in *Great Lives Observed: Louis XIV*, ed. John C. Rule (London, 1968). Another useful selection of source material, relating to all aspects of French politics and society during Louis XIV's lifetime, is *The Century of Louis XIV*, ed. Orest and Patricia Ranum (Harper Paperback edition, New York, 1972).

Specialised works

Chapter 1: Absolutism: theory and practice

For an excellent introduction, see:

Roger Mettam, 'France', in *Absolutism in Seventeenth-Century Europe*, ed. John Miller (London, 1990), pp. 43–67

The other essays in this volume also provide a very valuable European context for Louis XIV's régime.

There are further helpful discussions in:

A. Lossky, 'The Absolutism of Louis XIV: Reality or Myth?', *Canadian Journal of History* XIX (1984), 1–15

David Parker, *The Making of French Absolutism* (London, 1983), chapter 4

Herbert H. Rowen, 'Louis XIV and Absolutism', in *Louis XIV and the Craft of Kingship*, ed. Rule, pp. 302–16

A helpful survey of recent literature on this theme is presented in:

Richard Bonny, 'Absolutism: What's in a Name?', *French History* I (1987), 93–117

There is an intricate analysis of the workings of central government in:

R. Mettam, *Power and Faction in Louis XIV's France* (Oxford, 1988)

For an interesting exploration of the régime's impact on one particular province (Languedoc), see:

W. Beik, *Absolutism and Society in Seventeenth-Century France* (Cambridge, 1985)

A very stimulating discussion, which compares Louis XIV's rule with broader European developments, may be found in:

J. H. Shennan, *Liberty and Order in Early Modern Europe* (London, 1986), chapter 2

Chapter 2: Economic policies

Two useful overviews, setting Louis XIV's economic policies against the background of early modern Europe, are:

The Fontana Economic History of Europe: The Sixteenth and Seventeenth Centuries, ed. Carlo M. Cipolla (Glasgow, 1974)

Jan de Vries, *The Economy of Europe in an Age of Crisis, 1600–1750* (Cambridge, 1976)

There is a good introduction to Louis XIV's relations with Colbert in:

'The King and his Minister: Louis XIV and Colbert', *History Today* XIV (July 1964), 478–88

For more detailed studies of Colbert, see:

Andrew Trout, *Jean-Baptiste Colbert* (Boston, 1978)

Inès Murat, *Colbert*, trans. R.F. Cook and J. Van Asselt (Charlottesville, Virginia, 1984)

On the theories behind Colbert's policies, and the criticism which they aroused, see:

J. Meuvret, 'Fiscalism and Public Opinion under Louis XIV', in *Louis XIV and Absolutism*, ed. Hatton, pp. 199–225

Lionel Rothkrug, *Opposition to Louis XIV* (Princeton, New Jersey, 1965)

The fullest account of the condition of the French peasantry under Louis XIV is:

Pierre Goubert, *The French Peasantry in the Seventeenth Century*, trans. Ian Patterson (Cambridge, 1986)

Chapter 3: Social policies

For Louis XIV's treatment of the nobility, see:

R.R. Grassby, 'Social Status and Commercial Enterprise under Louis XIV', in *State and Society*, ed. Kierstead, pp. 200–32

Franklin L. Ford, *Robe and Sword: The Regrouping of the French Aristocracy after Louis XIV* (Harper Paperback edition, New York, 1965), chapter 1

The development of the French legal system is examined in:

A. Lloyd Moote, 'Law and Justice under Louis XIV', in *Louis XIV and the Craft of Kingship*, ed. Rule, pp. 224–39

J. H. Shennan, *The Parlement of Paris* (London, 1968)

There is a detailed account of the origins of the 1675 Breton revolt in:

John J. Hurst, 'The *Parlement* of Brittany and the Crown: 1665–1675', in *State and Society*, ed. Kierstead, pp. 44–66

For comparative material on other insurrections, see:

Leon Bernard, 'French Society and Popular Uprisings under Louis XIV', in *State and Society*, ed. Kierstead, pp. 157–79

Roland Mousnier, *Peasant Uprisings in Seventeenth-Century France, Russia and China*, trans. Brian Pearce (London, 1971), part I

Two books are especially valuable on the history of Paris in this period:

Leon Bernard, *The Emerging City: Paris in the Age of Louis XIV* (Durham, North Carolina, 1970)

O.A. Ranum, *Paris in the Age of Absolutism* (New York, 1968)

Chapter 4: Religious policies

Louis XIV's relations with the Catholic Church are examined in:

H.G. Judge, 'Church and State under Louis XIV', *History* XLV (1960), 217–33

H.G. Judge, 'Louis XIV and the Church', in *Louis XIV and the Craft of Kingship*, ed. Rule, pp. 240–64

The broader development of French Catholicism in this period is analysed in:

Jean Delumeau, *Catholicism between Luther and Voltaire*, trans. Jeremy Moiser (London, 1977)

For discussions of the revocation of the Edict of Nantes, see:
>Elisabeth Labrousse, 'Calvinism in France, 1598–1685'; and Philippe Joutard, 'The Revocation of the Edict of Nantes: End or Renewal of French Calvinism?'; both in *International Calvinism, 1541–1715*, ed. Menna Prestwich (Oxford, 1985), pp. 285–314 and 339–68
>J. Orcibal, 'Louis XIV and the Edict of Nantes', in *Louis XIV and Absolutism*, ed. Hatton, pp. 154–76

Chapter 5: Foreign policy

A useful survey, which sets Louis XIV's foreign policy in its European context, is:
>Jeremy Black, *The Rise of the European Powers, 1679–1793* (London, 1990), chapter 1

Good introductions to Louis XIV's general approach to foreign policy may be found in:
>John B. Wolf, 'Louis XIV, Soldier-King', in *Louis XIV and the Craft of Kingship*, ed. Rule, pp. 196–223
>V.-L. Tapié, 'Louis XIV's Methods in Foreign Policy', in *Louis XIV and Europe*, ed. Hatton, pp. 3–15
>A. Lossky, '"Maxims of State" in Louis XIV's Foreign Policy in the 1680s', in *William III and Louis XIV*, ed. Hatton and Bromley, pp. 7–23

On the policy of *réunions* and its consequences, the best studies are:
>G. Symcox, 'Louis XIV and the Outbreak of the Nine Years War', in *Louis XIV and Europe*, ed. Hatton, pp. 179–212
>Mark A. Thomson, 'Self-Determination and Collective Security as Factors in English and French Foreign Policy, 1689–1718', in *William III and Louis XIV*, ed. Hatton and Bromley, pp. 271–86

For the Partition Treaties and their diplomatic context, see:
>Mark A. Thomson, 'Louis XIV and the Origins of the War of the Spanish Succession', in *William III and Louis XIV*, ed. Hatton and Bromley, pp. 140–61

Chapter 6: Versailles: court and culture

An excellent overview of this topic may be found in:
>Ragnhild Hatton, 'Louis XIV: at the Court of the Sun King', in *The Courts of Europe*, ed. A.G. Dickens (London, 1977)

For two contrasting perspectives on the political significance of the Court, see:
>J. Levron, 'Louis XIV's Courtiers', in *Louis XIV and Absolutism*, ed. Hatton, pp. 130–53
>Nathan T. Whitman, 'Myth and Politics: Versailles and the Fountain of Latona', in *Louis XIV and the Craft of Kingship*, ed. Rule, pp. 286–301

On the cultural aspects of the Court, the following are particularly valuable:
>David Maland, *Culture and Society in Seventeenth-Century France* (London, 1970), chapters 8–9

Guy Walton, *Louis XIV's Versailles* (Harmondsworth, 1986)

R.M. Isherwood, *Music in the Service of the King* (Ithaca, 1972)

There are also two important analyses of the development of Louis XIV's public image in:

Louis Marin, *Portrait of the King*, trans. Martha M. Houle (Basingstoke, 1988)

Peter Burke, *The Fabrication of Louis XIV* (New Haven and London, 1992)

Index